The Contemporary Garden

The Contemporary Garden presents 100 seminal gardens from the early 1920s to the present day. The selection traces the development of the non-traditional and modern garden from the early experimentations of the twentieth century to the visionary ideas of today's practitioners. Organized chronologically, all types and styles are featured, including roof and water gardens, Modernist landscapes, conceptual installations and urban parks. This book presents the most influential and innovative designers, architects, land artists and horticulturalists through their best-known gardens, such as Fernando Caruncho's Wheat Garden in Spain and Tadao Ando's Garden of Fine Arts in Japan. Explore iconic gardens known the world over — from Joan Miró's Labyrinth to Nicholas Grimshaw's Eden Project — alongside more recent manifestations like Topher Delaney's 'In Line of Fire' garden. ***The Contemporary Garden*** is an inspiring guide to this ever-changing form.

La Thébaïde André & Paul Vera

The box-edged flower garden designed by the brothers Vera for their country retreat at Saint-Germain-en-Laye is perhaps the most honest reconciliation ever made in garden design between classicism and modernity. André Vera subscribed to the seventeenth-century view that a garden should be 'a refined version of nature …

nature shaped into intelligible forms'. But he argued for a modernized version of this formal approach that allowed for painterly use of bright colours and modern materials, such as concrete. This was also a patriotic celebration of the optimism of post-war France — Vera suggested the use of native French plants instead of exotic imports.

In their designs — a public garden at Honfleur or the modern parterre garden at the Paris house of Charles and Marie-Laure de Noailles — the Veras sought to honour the French gardening tradition while making it relevant to modern circumstances.

La Thébaïde, Saint-Germain-en-Laye, France, 1920. André Vera. b Paris, France, 1881. d Saint-Germain-en-Laye, France, 1971. Paul Vera. b Paris, France, 1882. d Saint-Germain-en-Laye, France, 1957.   4

Tachard Garden Pierre-Emile Legrain

A formal Modernist *allée* zigzags through the garden made for African art collector Jeanne Tachard. Its cool, ordered dignity, which is nevertheless both asymmetrical and irregular, exemplifies the style of this now-vanished garden. Pierre-Emile Legrain was a leading designer of the 1910s and 1920s, specializing in interiors, furniture and books.

This is the only garden he designed. Legrain's scheme was original in its deliberately inconclusive use of irregular geometric forms and changes of level, designed to create varying tones of green and to emphasize the textures of plants. The scheme comprises a series of garden rooms, including an outdoor dining area, in which the impersonal

formal style is undercut by playfully off-beat, off-centre motifs. Legrain was unusual among his Modernist contemporaries in his sympathy for and understanding of plants: the Tachard garden included a voluptuous semicircle of red climbing roses that he described as 'a sacrifice to charm'.

Tachard Garden, La Celle-Saint-Cloud, France, 1924. **Pierre-Emile Legrain**. b Levallois-Perret, France, 1889. d Paris, France, 1929.

Villa Bomsel André Lurçat

This garden at the Villa Bomsel, seen here from the second floor of the house, was one of several doomed attempts in the 1920s and 1930s to create a prototype garden suited to Modernist architecture. André Lurçat's design comprised an irregular geometric parterre of cut turf and flowers, bisected by gravel paths and a water *allée* lined with sword lilies. Lurçat intended the garden to be viewed primarily from above (there is no access from the ground floor) and attempted to unify the house with the garden through the use of materials. As part of this plan, he used slabs of concrete for the water features and benches, and as decorative elements in their own right. Unusually among his Modernist contemporaries, Lurçat demonstrated an interest in horticulture: the light-blue concrete slabs were adorned with climbing roses and espaliered fruit trees lined the walls.

Villa Bomsel, Versailles, France, 1924. **André Lurçat**. b Bruyères, Vosges, France, 1894. d Sceaux, Hauts-de-Seine, France, 1970.

Garden with Concrete Trees Robert Mallet-Stevens

The landscape section of the 1925 Paris Exposition, supervised by French landscape architect J C N Forestier (1861–1930), contained the most avant-garde designs of the century, among the usual homages to tradition or exotic international style. Encouraged to experiment with new materials, Robert Mallet-Stevens championed concrete, creating a series of ornaments and buildings for the Exposition, including this garden with concrete trees. Concrete retaining walls created four raised beds enclosing simple arrangements of planes of grass and sempervivum. Each bed was ornamented with a tall concrete tree made by Jan and Joël Martel, who attached branches (slabs of concrete) to a central concrete trunk. Serious-minded Modernists praised the garden, but there was some hilarity among the press and public, with speculation that the real trees for the garden had died. This showpiece was probably the most uncompromising Modernist garden ever created.

Garden with Concrete Trees, Paris Exposition, France, 1925. **Robert Mallet-Stevens**. b Paris, France, 1886. d Paris, France, 1945.

Naumkeag Fletcher Steele

Mabel Choate's request for some simple steps to help her climb the slope to her vegetable garden at Naumkeag, Massachusetts, produced an icon of twentieth-century garden design. In the Blue Steps, created in the 1920s, Fletcher Steele interpreted a classic Renaissance form in a strikingly modern way. A series of blue-painted concrete arches, flanked by double flights of stairs and sweeping Art Deco-style railings, climb between the gleaming white trunks of silver birches. The birches contrast beautifully with the symmetry of the architecture. Water cascades through the arches as in an Italian water staircase. Steele had a classical Beaux-Arts training but admired the contemporary French garden designers Vera, Legrain and Guévrékian. He worked at Naumkeag (an Indian word meaning 'Haven of Peace') from 1925 until the late 1950s, adding an eclectic range of features, including a Chinese pagoda and moon gate, a green garden and a rose garden of scalloped beds.

Naumkeag, Stockbridge, MA, USA, 1925. **Fletcher Steele**. b Rochester, NY, USA, 1885. d New York, NY, USA, 1971.

Villa Noailles Gabriel Guévrékian

The only survivor, albeit rebuilt, of the French Modernist garden movement of the 1920s and 1930s, the Cubist garden at the Villa Noailles was commissioned by Vicomte and Vicomtesse de Noailles after they had seen Gabriel Guévrékian's show garden at the 1925 Paris Exposition. The garden is an abstract, geometric composition with a dynamic forward thrust, a complement to the Modernist house by Robert Mallet-Stevens. Guévrékian's original design specified tulips at the point of the triangle and in alternate squares of the interlocking geometric design. Orange trees were planted where the box balls now are and an automated abstract sculpture was a focus at the garden's apex. The garden works as a still-life tableau viewed from above, and also as a three-dimensional space where multiple viewpoints are gradually discovered, as in a Cubist painting. In the same year, Guévrékian designed a garden of terraced Modernist compartments at the Villa Heim in Neuilly-sur-Seine, but such commissions were rare.

Villa Noailles, Hyères, France, 1926. **Gabriel Guévrékian**. b Istanbul, Turkey, 1900. d Antibes, France, 1970.

German Pavilion Ludwig Mies van der Rohe

A nude gestures across the expanse of this shallow marble-lined pool. Building it on a 53.6 by 17 m (175 by 56 ft) travertine platform, Ludwig Mies van der Rohe designed the German Pavilion at the Barcelona International Exhibition of 1929 to have a very minimal structure of cruciform steel columns, with a flat overhanging roof and glass and honey-coloured onyx walls. It is the prime twentieth-century example of the seamless integration of exterior and interior spaces — the pool shown is mirrored by an even larger shallow pool lined with pebbles on the entrance side of the pavilion. The glass walls seem to disappear, exemplifying the famous phrase ascribed to Mies, 'less is more'. Mies was the director of the Bauhaus in Germany but emigrated to the USA in 1937. He was one of the most important architects of the twentieth century, responsible for many Modern movement buildings, including the Seagram Building in New York and the Farnsworth House in Plano, Illinois.

German Pavilion (Barcelona Pavilion), Montjuic, Barcelona, Spain, 1929, restored 1986. **Ludwig Mies van der Rohe (Ludwig Mies)**. b Aachen, Germany, 1886. d Chicago, IL, USA, 1969.

Sutton Courtenay Norah Lindsay

Norah Lindsay's own words, 'Without grandeur, but not without formality', written in 1931, capture the essence of the haphazard luxuriance of her timeless garden with its spires of topiary rising above the small clumps of perennials. Yet despite the apparent gay abandon, Lindsay, who was a disciple of and natural successor to Gertrude Jekyll, carefully orchestrated the colour scheme and arrangement of plant form and foliage. However, true to her romantic nature and view that gardening was dramatic theatre, Lindsay allowed the display to be supplemented by self-sown seedlings which succeeded in 'claiming squatter's rights'. Her innate sense of style and good taste won her a list of wealthy clients in the 1920s and 1930s, including the Astors at Cliveden and Lord Lothian at Blickling. She was also a close friend of Lawrence Johnston, creator of Hidcote, and helped him plan his 'jungle of beauty', her natural flamboyance a perfect foil to his inherent shyness.

Villa Savoye Le Corbusier

This solarium roof terrace at the Villa Savoye was designed for health-giving nude sunbathing. Le Corbusier, probably the most influential figure in twentieth-century Modernist architecture, regarded the roof or balcony terrace as the proper place for a garden, and practised a non-interventionist approach to the wider landscape.

At the Villa Savoye, a limited palette of plants, mainly evergreen shrubs, adorn raised beds in a series of terraces that lead directly on to the interior living areas. The outside is as important a designed space as the inside. Le Corbusier cited the Islamic tradition as an inspiration for the episodic progression here. Distant

prospects — in this case, groups of trees — were incorporated into the design by means of formal framing. Le Corbusier designed several such roof terraces, as well as a few gardens on the ground (the Villa Church and the Villa 'Les Terrasses'), where winding paths lead through trees to formal paved areas.

Villa Savoye, Poissy, France, 1928–31. **Le Corbusier (Charles-Edouard Jeanneret)**. b La Chaux-de-Fonds, Switzerland, 1887. d Cap Martin, France, 1965.

Rockefeller Center Roof Gardens Dr David Hosack

A thousand office windows look onto what must be the most dramatic roof garden in the world, atop the Rockefeller Center on 5th Avenue in New York. There are in fact four gardens in a row, identical to this one, incorporated into the Rockefeller Center's design. Ralph Hancock installed the gardens in 1933, apparently in line with the wishes of one Dr David Hosack, the botanist owner–founder of the Elgin Botanical Gardens that had occupied the site on which the Center is built, who envisaged a Hanging Gardens of Babylon for New York. The design is a kind of international formal, a mixture of Italian, French and English influences, with clipped pyramid yews, box hedges, a square pool and compartments for flowers. Since the gardens were part of the building's original design, there is a 60 cm (2 ft) depth of soil throughout. A good place from which to view the Rockefeller Gardens is the seventh-floor café in Saks, 5th Avenue.

Rockefeller Center Roof Gardens, New York, NY, USA, 1933. **Dr David Hosack**. **b** New York, NY, USA, 1769. **d** New York, NY, USA, 1835.

Târgu Jiu Sculpture Park Constantin Brancusi

In a vast wooded park designed for meditation and remembrance *The Table of Silence*, a circular limestone slab surrounded by twelve seats, sits as if suspended in time. Further down the central *allée*, *The Gate of Kiss* and *The Endless Column* complete this remarkable ensemble of sculptures. Constantin Brancusi designed both park and sculptures, creating a highly spiritual environment reminiscent of ancient stone alignments. A pioneer of abstraction, he was one of the first modern sculptors to be interested in the relationship between his art and the environment, suggesting the idea of an ever-changing work of art following the viewers' perspective. Commissioned by the Romanian state, Târgu Jiu Sculpture Park was built in 1938. Its site is close to Brancusi's native home in Romania, although he had not lived there since 1903, when he crossed the whole of Europe on foot to reach Paris.

Târgu Jiu Sculpture Park, Târgu Jiu, Gorj, Romania, 1938. **Constantin Brancusi**. b Hobitza, Gorj, Romania, 1876. d Paris, France, 1957.

Bentley Wood Christopher Tunnard

This garden at Halland in East Sussex was one of a small handful of commissions that Christopher Tunnard, the torch-bearer for the Modernist garden in Britain, received in the 1930s. In his 1938 manifesto, *Gardens in the Modern Landscape*, he railed at informal gardens of herbaceous colour: 'The present-day garden, with the sixpenny novelette, is a last stronghold of romanticism.' Halland featured a large paved terrace all round the Modernist house by Serge Chermayeff, which is on the south side, boldly extended via a straight, narrow path that leads to another terrace with a rectangular grid framing the landscape. It was here, on the platform to the right of the steps, that Tunnard envisaged the placement of a sculpture by Henry Moore. Indeed, Moore's *Recumbent Figure* was briefly installed. Tunnard's example was largely ignored in practical terms, and in the 1940s he moved to the United States to teach at Harvard and Yale, where he continued to publish work on the Modern movement.

Bentley Wood, Halland, Lewes, East Sussex, UK, c1938. **Christopher Tunnard**. b Victoria, BC, Canada, 1910. d New York, NY, USA, 1979.

Fallingwater Frank Lloyd Wright

Deep in the Pennsylvania forest, hovering above the bed of a mighty waterfall, the house seems to emanate from the landscape like a natural outcrop. Fallingwater is perhaps one of the best-known modern private houses in the world and is undoubtedly one of Frank Lloyd Wright's best works. This 1935 commission for a weekend retreat for the Philadelphia department-store owner E J Kaufman marked a turning point in Wright's career and stretched his art beyond even his previous work, the influential 'prairie house'. Here the house is so at one with the elements and the landscape that it doesn't actually allow the mental perception of physical space that defines a garden. In its groundbreaking newness Fallingwater is a primeval reference to the essence of both man and nature. It refers back to a time when the cultural space of the garden made no sense, where no transition was needed between human habitation and the wilderness. The wilderness itself was man's garden.

Fallingwater, Bear Run, PA, USA, 1935–9. **Frank Lloyd Wright**. **b** Richland Center, WI, USA, 1867. **d** Phoenix, AZ, USA, 1959.

Tofuku-ji Mirei Shigemori

A field of white sand, finely raked in a criss-cross pattern, fills a transitional space in the Tofuku-ji gardens. Of the four modern gardens redesigned in 1939, after a fire ruined the Zen monastery, the most famous is the South Garden. There, on the patterned white gravel, four groups of large rocks form a striking vertical/horizontal composition, while five low mossy mounds crouch in the opposite corner. Though the classical syntax of Japanese gardens is followed almost to the letter, a profound sense of modernity and individuality reigns is this masterpiece by Mirei Shigemori. His immense influence was compounded by his authority as a historian and theoretician. Shigemori argued that, after centuries of inspired and supreme mastery, Japanese garden design fell into decline when it became the attribute of professional designers. To counteract the subsequent dryness and emptiness, Shigemori returned the garden to its original status as an integral and specific work of art, never to be repeated or copied.

Tofuku-ji, Kyoto, Japan, 1939. **Mirei Shigemori**. b Okyama, Japan, 1896. d Kyoto, Japan, 1975.

Villa Mairea Alvar Aalto

Inscribed in a simple forest clearing, an asymmetrical pool recalls the contours of a lake. The timber screen of the porch on the villa reflects the rhythms of the tree trunks in the forest. This stunning design, which is simultaneously organic and modern, is extended inside the villa with, for example, the irregular staircase balustrade which echoes the view out on to the forest. The design of the Villa Mairea and its garden refers to the metaphorical opposition between artificial and natural forms, as well as to the energy that originates from their union. Much admired since its completion in 1939, the Villa Mairea constitutes a link between the national Finnish Romantic tradition and the Rational-Constructivist Movement of the early twentieth century, to which the architect and designer Alvar Aalto was committed. Apart from his numerous furniture designs, Aalto realized over 200 buildings in his lifetime which makes him the second most productive architect of the twentieth century, after Frank Lloyd Wright.

Villa Mairea, Noormarkku, Finland, 1937–9. **Alvar Aalto**. **b** Kuortane, Finland, 1898. **d** Helsinki, Finland, 1976.

Perry Green Henry Moore

Now so familiar as to be almost commonplace, the sight of monumental, smooth bronze sculptures lying in a field was once a daring innovation. If today the relationship between the modern, three-dimensional object of art and a natural fold of the landscape seems an obvious one, it is partly due to the influence of Henry Moore. When in 1940 he and his

wife Irina left London and their house in Hampstead, which had been damaged in a bombing, they headed for the small village of Perry Green in Hertfordshire. There they lived until the end of their lives, progressively adding buildings and land to the original cottage and sheep field. Irina was particularly active in transforming the grounds.

She created a series of gardens and less formal settings where the sculptures could be displayed in a flexible and open manner. Moore himself sited some large pieces, while other displays were meant to be temporary.

Perry Green, The Henry Moore Foundation, Much Hadham, Hertfordshire, UK, 1940. **Henry Moore. b** Castleford, Yorkshire, UK, 1898. **d** Much Hadham, Hertfordshire, UK, 1986.

Woodland Cemetery Erik Gunnar Asplund & Sigurd Lewerentz

Hidden away in dense woodland, a modest chapel awaits the mourners. The surrounding spruces are over twice its height and they are echoed in the twelve simple concrete columns of the anteroom. Further on, the landscape dramatically opens into a vast expanse of grass sweeping towards an artificial hill on which stands a monumental cross. This deliberately biblical landscape is completed by a modernistic temple-like hall and by the Faith, Hope and Charity chapels. A profound sense of balance and peace emanates from the landscaped complex at the Stockholm cemetery. Here the geometric framework of Modernism blends happily with the intrinsic values of the landscape. Asplund and Lewerentz are widely recognized as two of the few architects of the early twentieth century to have achieved this synthesis. At that time garden-makers and the first ecologists tended to reject modern architecture, while modern architects shunned the models of the traditional home and garden.

Woodland Cemetery, Enskede, Stockholm, Sweden, 1917–40. **Erik Gunnar Asplund**. b Stockholm, Sweden, 1885. d Stockholm, Sweden, 1940.
Sigurd Lewerentz. b Sandö, Sweden, 1885. d Lund, Sweden, 1975.

Tulcán Gardens José Maria Azuel Franco Guerrero

Some of the most elaborate topiary in the world has been produced by an untrained genius in Tulcán, a small Andean city in Ecuador. In the early 1940s, Franco Guerrero began to clip hedges of Arizona cypress, *Cupressus arizonica*, located in the town cemetery, into a variety of geometric, anthropomorphic and zoomorphic forms. Arranged in avenues along the cemetery's walks or outdoor garden 'rooms' are myriads of clipped shapes. There are truncated cones, pyramids, obelisks and arches and bas-reliefs of architectural mouldings as well as human, animal and bird-like forms. There are also portraits of heroes drawn from South American, Oriental and Egyptian mythology.

The inspiration for the incised modelling of these forms can be traced to the stone-carving style of the pre-Columbian cultures of Ecuador. The art of twentieth-century topiary has reached an apogee in this remote South American town.

Tulcán Gardens, Tulcán, Ecuador, 1940s. **José Maria Azuel Franco Guerrero**. b Tulcán, Ecuador, 1907. d Tulcán, Ecuador, 1985.

Dartington Hall Percy Cane

In the Tiltyard at Dartington Hall in Devon, terraced grass banks, a broad York stone stairway and clipped yew hedges combine in a poetic interplay of geometric forms, sharply defined by sunlight and shadow, and contrasting dramatically with the surrounding trees. It is one of the world's most distinctive garden landscapes, located in one of Britain's most magical gardens. Grandeur — as seen in the Tiltyard — is combined with the intimacy of quiet woodland walks, a secluded meadow and a rustic gardener's cottage. Dating back to the fourteenth century, Dartington Hall was built for Richard II's half-brother, John Holland. The present garden is largely the work of Percy Cane, a prolific designer whose clients included Haile Selassie. Cane was commissioned by Dorothy and Leonard Elmhirst, who acquired the estate in 1925 and founded the experimental College of Arts. He followed two other consultants used by the Elmhirsts — the American Beatrix Farrand and Harry Avray Tipping.

Dartington Hall, Totnes, Devon, UK, from 1945. **Percy (Stephen Percival) Cane**. b Braintree, Essex, UK, 1881. d Wallingford, Oxfordshire, UK, 1976.

El Novillero Thomas Church

This free-form pool designed by Thomas Church was inspired by the beautiful curved shores of the bay and the work of Alvar Aalto. It became an icon of twentieth-century landscape design. When it was built, its biomorphic shape was revolutionary. The image of this pool transformed the way swimming pools were designed, firstly in California and then across the States over the next thirty years. Church was commissioned to design the pool and the surrounding terraces shaded by evergreen holm oaks at the northern end of San Francisco Bay by Mr and Mrs Donnell, who built a house on the site in the 1940s. The property is still owned by the Donnell family today. Through his work, and his book *Gardens are for People*, Church encouraged the wider public to visualize a real use of space based on a twentieth-century modern design aesthetic. Church also mastered the deck design for small gardens.

El Novillero, Sonoma, CA, USA, 1947–9. **Thomas Church**. b Boston, MA, USA, 1902. d San Francisco, CA, USA, 1978.

Lincoln Memorial Garden Jens Jensen

This quiet glade of spring-flowering trees set in a public park is the epitome of Jens Jensen's style as a landscape architect and designer. The garden became a living memorial to Abraham Lincoln, most illustrious son of Illinois, and Jensen — an émigré from Denmark — waived his fee when he worked on the project from 1936 to 1949.

Because many of the species he wanted were unavailable commercially, Illinois school children and garden clubs collected acorns, seeds and wild plants from woodland areas before they were cleared. Volunteers planted thousands of acorns, hundreds of saplings and all the wild plants into the series of open spaces between the wood

that Jensen had designed. He was best known for his plantings of indigenous species and he evolved the Prairie Style of landscape and garden design, which was sympathetic to the contemporary Midwest school of architecture, Prairie School, led by the great Frank Lloyd Wright, with whom Jensen collaborated on some projects.

Lincoln Memorial Garden, Springfield, IL, USA, 1936–49. **Jens Jensen**. **b** Dybbøl, Denmark, 1860. **d** Ellison Bay, WI, USA, 1951.

Rock Garden Nek Chand Saini

Frozen in the rigidity of their steel armatures, coated with tightly packed rags, crowds of statues and herds of animals populate the clearings, waterfalls and temples of the Rock Garden at Chandigarh, one of the world's most poignant and spectacular visionary environments. As is often the case with extraordinary places, their genesis is equally remarkable. In the 1950s, Nek Chand Saini was a civil servant employed on the huge building site which was the new city of Chandigarh — an extraordinary project designed by Le Corbusier. But Chand had a dream. Collecting stones and waste material from the tons of rubble from the twenty villages razed to make way for the new city, he secretly started designing his dream kingdom in a clearing behind his state-owned dwelling. Support for Chand's great work grew so strong that the authorities were compelled to offer men and means to allow Chand to complete his dream. Now covering 20 hectares (50 acres), it receives over 5,000 visitors a day.

Rock Garden, Chandigarh, India, 1950s. **Nek Chand Saini**. b Barian Kalan, nr Shakargarh Tehsil, Punjab, Pakistan, 1924.

Regatta Restaurant Garden Frank Clark & Maria Shephard

Frank Clark was a member of the generation of British landscape and garden designers who endured the stymied, retrospective styles that epitomized the 1930s, only to come into his own in the post-1945 era. Appointed landscape consultant of the Festival of Britain, Clark and émigré Italian designer Maria Teresa Parpagliolo Shephard designed this garden to complement Misha Black's innovative Regatta Restaurant building. With its abstract free form, the informal use of rock and gravel (building materials not subject to rationing), plantings of sculptural specimen shrubs, ground cover and sinuous-edged pool were complemented by Lynn Chadwick's abstract bronze sculpture. Taken together with Sir Peter Shepheard's Moat Garden, this was the first British expression of a modern garden on a suburban scale. The style became popular because it was inexpensive to achieve, easily attainable and worked well in a small space, requiring little maintenance.

The Regatta Restaurant Garden, Festival of Britain Gardens, London, UK, 1951. **Frank Clark**. b Manila, The Philippines, 1902. d UK, 1971.
Maria Teresa Parpagliolo Shephard. b Rome, Italy, 1913. d UK, 2002.

University of Aarhus Carl Theodor Sørensen

This amphitheatre was Carl Theodor Sørensen's design solution to a change in level on the site at the University of Aarhus, Denmark. The screen between the amphitheatre and the university buildings is of oak trees. Sørensen's vision was to create a university set in an oak grove. Over the course of his career, Sørensen designed six green

amphitheatres in Denmark, each of them slightly different. Concentric circles were among many geometric forms that he used repeatedly in a career spanning over 2,000 commissions. As well as public sites like this campus, he designed many smaller gardens. His broad range as a designer, and his work as a teacher and author, earned

him a reputation as the father of modern landscape architecture in Denmark and an influence throughout Scandinavia. He is also credited with the invention of the adventure playground, which he explored in his book *Park Politics in Parish and Borough*, written in 1931.

University of Aarhus, Aarhus, Denmark, 1931–53. **Carl Theodor Sørensen**. **b** Altona, Germany, 1893. **d** Copenhagen, Denmark, 1979.

MoMA Courtyard Sculpture Garden Philip Johnson

The courtyard of the Museum of Modern Art in New York is more than a display space for modern sculpture; the works seem to 'live' there very happily and there is a sense, when entering this garden, of coming into the sculptures' very own space. A simple design of canals, stone perimeters and walkways, together with sober plantings, creates an impression of space and balance, while providing the necessary seclusion. Yoshio Taniguchi's redesign of the museum in 2004 preserved the original garden for this courtyard. At the time of its commission, in 1953, Philip Johnson was a trustee of the museum and the director of the architecture department. Having initially studied philosophy at Harvard, he suddenly changed direction in his thirties after reading the writings of Mies van der Rohe, Le Corbusier and Walter Gropius. Johnson's International Style (as it came to be known) and, in particular, his daring skyscrapers left their mark on many North American city skylines.

MoMA Courtyard Sculpture Garden (The Abby Aldrich Rockefeller Sculpture Garden), New York, NY, USA, 1953. Philip Johnson. b New London, OH, USA, 1906. d New Canaan, CT, USA, 2005.

The James Rose Center James Rose

Beautifully finished, raised natural wooden floors and *shoji* screens are but two of the Japanese influences on the designs made by James Rose in 1954 for his own house and garden in Ridgewood, New Jersey. This style was inspired by time spent in the Pacific during World War II. Rose's garden spaces are seen as interlinked volumes, often divided by transparent screens. Woven wooden fencing allows glimpses into adjacent spaces. Rose called the garden 'the gateless gate of Zen Buddhism'. His designs depended on the changing character and fleeting nature of the effects of light, shadow, sound, space and texture. The tradition of the Orient allied to the modernity of the Bauhaus espoused at Harvard in the late 1930s, where Rose, Garrett Eckbo and Dan Kiley rebelled against the Beaux-Arts fashion, radically changed professional landscape design philosophies both in the United States and in a wider, international context.

The James Rose Center, Ridgewood, NJ, USA, 1954. **James C Rose**. b Matamoras, PA, USA, 1913. d Ridgewood, NJ, USA, 1991.

J Irwin Miller Residence Dan Kiley

Henry Moore's *Seated Woman* reclines gracefully at the end of an immaculate *allée* of honey locusts (*Gleditsia triacanthos*) planted across the western edge of the house. Completed in 1955, this was Dan Kiley's first coherently modern landscape design, incorporating the 'rich vocabulary of *allée*, *bosquet*, boulevard and *tapis vert*'

encountered in post-war Europe, where he had helped to reconstruct Nuremberg's Palace of Justice. Around the house the spaces are ordered and geometric: a redbud grove next to the Moore sculpture interlocks with blocks of apple orchards, lawn, avenued entrance drive and swimming pool, the whole enclosed by staggered

arborvitae hedges. A master among American landscape architects, Kiley embraced Modernism in the 1930s. After his European epiphany, he strove to build 'landscapes of clarity and infinity', repeating classical elements in a modern composition.

J Irwin Miller Residence, Columbus, IA, USA, 1955. **Dan Kiley (Daniel Urban Kiley)**. b Boston, MA, USA, 1912. d Charlotte, VT, USA, 2004.

The Gibberd Garden Sir Frederick Gibberd

In this twentieth-century garden of surprises, massive columns in Portland stone and marshalled Coade-stone urns rise from a wild planting of acanthus. Improbably, the statuary came from Coutts Bank in London's Strand, incorporated by the master-planner of Harlow New Town into his eclectic sculpture garden. Gibberd moved here in 1956, inheriting a soaring avenue of limes, a gazebo and a formal pool. Over the years he developed a series of interlocking walled spaces near the house and intimate garden enclosures for his growing collection of sculptures, most of which were modern, as well as play features for his grandchildren. 'I consulted the genius of the place,' he said, 'and then exercised some intuition, without which no art exists.' Within an essentially informal English garden of 2.8 hectares (7 acres), Gibberd introduced an architect's masterly manipulation of space, adding drama to each of his sculptures. After several years of quiet neglect, the garden has been restored by the Gibberd Garden Trust.

The Gibberd Garden, Harlow, Essex, UK, from 1956. **Sir Frederick Ernest Gibberd**. b Coventry, West Midlands, UK, 1908. d Harlow, Essex, UK, 1984.

UNESCO Foundation Sculpture Garden Isamu Noguchi

Near a pool, a stone arrangement in the motif of Horai stands below a gently undulating ridge planted with pines and maples. The garden, encircled by Marcel Breuer's Modernist architecture, acts as a sea of perfect quietude. When commissioned in 1956 to make a garden for the UNESCO headquarters in Paris, Isamu Noguchi was at the height of his popularity as a sculptor. He viewed this both as a challenge to embrace the art of garden-making, and as an opportunity to fuse his own Modernist design style with the ancient principles of Japanese garden art which so fascinated him. To re-energize his bonds with that tradition, he went twice to Japan. There he met the great designer Mirei Shigemori who took him to the island of Shikoku to select and extract stones to be shipped to Paris. Though considered 'the pre-eminent American sculptor' of his time by Robert Hughes, Noguchi really belonged to both cultures, taking on the best of each.

UNESCO Foundation Sculpture Garden, Paris, France, 1956–8. Isamu Noguchi. b Los Angeles, CA, USA, 1904. d New York, NY, USA, 1988.

Alcoa Forecast Garden Garrett Eckbo

An arrangement of vertical and horizontal panels in tinted aluminium creates an intriguing inside–outdoor transition from the house to a luxuriant garden, planted with sub-tropical plants. The Aluminum Forecast House was a 1959 experiment by Alcoa Aluminum to explore the use of their products in garden designs. Eckbo used his own house in Laurel Canyon, Los Angeles, for the experiment. Eckbo was a major influence on landscape architecture throughout his long career, engaging with social and technological innovations in his own work and in collaboration with some of the most important architects of the time. He studied at Harvard with James Rose and Dan Kiley, and all three were influenced by the Modern Movement architect Walter Gropius. Early in his career, Eckbo participated in social and agricultural experiments during the New Deal. His *Landscape for Living* and *The Landscape We See*, along with his teaching at Berkeley, helped revolutionize modern American landscape

Alcoa Forecast Garden, Laurel Canyon, Los Angeles, CA, USA, 1959. **Garrett Eckbo**. **b** Cooperstown, NY, USA, 1910. **d** Oakland, CA, USA, 2000.

McIntyre Garden Lawrence Halprin

This Modernist garden contrasts solid, non-organic forms with the essence of nature: its sounds, smells and textures. Loosely based on traditional Spanish patio design — running water in geometric channels, enclosure and an emphasis on a limited number of trees and plants — the garden is low-maintenance and its layout encourages curiosity. Low walls screen water features which can be heard but not seen until another route through the garden is followed. In this way, movement through the space is encouraged, echoing the movement of the water. Lawrence Halprin began his career as an apprentice in the office of Thomas Church in 1945, and was his assistant at El Novillero. The McIntyre Garden was Halprin's first large-scale commission and many of its ideas were to be incorporated, on an even larger scale, for major waterfalls, plazas and parks in some of his high-profile projects, such as the Franklin Delano Roosevelt Memorial in Washington and Lovejoy Plaza in Portland.

McIntyre Garden, Bay Area, CA, USA, 1960. **Lawrence Halprin**. **b** New York, NY, USA, 1916.

Mount Cuba Residence Pamela Copeland & Dr Richard Lighty

Dappled woodland light falls on candelabra primula and native American phlox. Mount Cuba's garden addresses one of the great questions of contemporary gardening — the relationship between conservation and gardening. Pamela Copeland was awakened to the need to conserve land for wild flowers by the steady depletion of the

Delaware wildlands. During the 1960s, she acquired a meadow and woodland adjacent to her garden and the new area was developed with the advice and supervision of Dr Richard Lighty. Its planting is limited mainly to the native plants of the Piedmont mountain chain which runs north–south through the Delaware

region. Only occasionally are exotic plants used to enliven the garden visually. Using approximately 300 native plant species, the garden is planted not only for conservation but also for aesthetic effect, which changes annually as controlled self-seeding of the wild flowers is encouraged.

Mount Cuba Residence, DE, USA, 1960s. **Pamela Cunningham Copeland**. b Litchfield, CT, USA, 1906. d Wilmington, DE, USA, 2001. **Dr Richard Lighty**. b USA, 1933.

Kröller-Müller Sculpture Park Jan Bijhouwer

Dancing with its own reflection, a white sculpture by Hungarian artist Marta Pan floats on a small pond. This 1960 special commission was created by the artist as 'a meeting point between sky and water', taking into account the surrounding lawns, trees and paths. Placed with equal precision, dozens of other sculptures are dotted around the Otterlo park of the Kröller-Müller Museum. The idea of siting modern sculptures outdoors was present right from the beginning, in the 1930s, when the enterprising and wealthy Kröller-Müller couple created their museum. When it opened to the public in 1961, Otterlo was one of the very first sculpture parks. F D Hammacher, director of the museum, had by then commissioned the renowned landscape architect Jan Bijhouwer to design a landscape with open places and secluded spots, lawns and pools. These areas were then 'curated' as in any art gallery. In 2002, the landscape architects group West 8 renovated the park to expand and re-emphasize its original design.

Kröller-Müller Sculpture Park, Otterlo, nr Amsterdam, The Netherlands, 1961, renovated 2002. **Jan Bijhouwer**. b Amsterdam, The Netherlands, 1898. d The Netherlands, 1974.

Templemere Ivor Cunningham & Preben Jakobsen

Templemere is a typical Span development of 65 houses set in 5 hectares (12.5 acres) of artfully designed grounds with a lake surrounded by woodland. Established in 1948, with Eric Lyons as consultant architect, Span's mission was to span 'the gap between the suburban monotony of the typical speculative development and the architecturally designed, individually built residence that has become … financially unattainable'. These affordable houses are designed along Modernist principles with full awareness of how people live. Crucial to the concept was landscape architect Ivor Cunningham. He joined the team in 1955 and worked with Lyons to set the houses in harmony with the site (for example, retaining as many trees as possible) and to conceive designs that united private and public space: the houses defining the setting, and the setting enhancing the houses. Preben Jakobsen, who joined Span in 1961, contributed detailed planting to Cunningham's layouts. The results have been acclaimed by critics ever since.

Templemere Estate and Garden, Weybridge, Surrey, UK, 1963. **Ivor Cunningham**. b Orpington, Kent, UK, 1928. d Orpington, Kent, UK, 2007. **Preben Jakobsen**. b Denmark, 1934.

Turn End Peter Aldington

At Turn End, the house that he designed for his own use, Peter Aldington realized a happy transition from house to garden via an enclosed courtyard, which also encloses a pool and gnarled *Robinia pseudoacacia*. The fact that the three houses and their gardens at the Turn End development were designed as a piece by the same architect, and that this was considered revolutionary even in the 1960s, is symptomatic of the classic division between the landscape and architectural professions. Aldington is an accomplished and imaginative gardener as well as a Modernist architect. The half-acre grounds are packed with incident and feature several separate areas, including a daisy garden and a formal box courtyard planted each year with different brightly coloured annuals. A variety of mature shrubs and trees provides a setting for sculptures. A gravelled area called No-Mans is intensively gardened, with herbaceous perennials, grasses, troughs of alpines and pans of houseleeks.

Turn End, Haddenham, Aylesbury, Buckinghamshire, UK, 1964. **Peter Aldington**. **b** Preston, Lancashire, UK, 1933.

Villa il Roseto Pietro Porcinai

A graceful modern parterre gently slopes away from the house towards the town of Fiesole. Beneath it, a room of imposing proportions, bathed in dappled daylight, serves as the main entrance to the property and underground car park. With concrete columns and cupolas, geometrically decorated floor and walls, it is a modern reinterpretation of

the underground grottoes of the sixteenth and seventeenth centuries. This design innovation is typical of Pietro Porcinai's capacity to find workable solutions to modern situations and denotes his striking ability to translate the essential characteristics of the Italian tradition into contemporary aesthetics. He applied these qualities to

many private gardens in Europe, the Middle East, North and South America, but also on larger projects such as the Brenner motorway. The fact that he was brought up at the Tuscan villa of La Gamberaia, where his father was head gardener, helps explain his fluency and the confidence of his instincts.

Villa il Roseto, Fiesole, Florence, Italy, 1961–5. **Pietro Porcinai**. b Florence, Italy, 1910. d Florence, Italy, 1986.

Little Sparta Ian Hamilton Finlay

A quotation from the French revolutionary Saint-Just is a highlight of the literary garden created in Scotland by the 'concrete poet' Ian Hamilton Finlay. Since 1966 and until his death in 2006, Hamilton Finlay adorned the garden with buildings, statues and inscribed stone tablets with deep classical resonances. The emblems and maxims of the leading thinkers of the French Revolution, who championed ancient Roman virtues, as well as Rousseau and his philosophy of the simple pastoral life, are repeated in features that adorn the mown paths, woodland glades and open vistas. The garden is implicitly a critique of contemporary cultural values. In 1978 Finlay was involved in a tax dispute with the local authority and the garden was mobilized as if for artistic war, with hand grenades and battleships now enriching its decoration. The dispute also led to the renaming of the garden, which was originally called Stonypath. Finlay contributed inscribed stones to gardens and parks all over Europe.

Little Sparta, Dunsyre, Lanarkshire, UK, 1966–2006. **Ian Hamilton Finlay**. **b** Nassau, Bahamas, 1925. **d** Edinburgh, UK, 2006.

Kiraç Villa Sedad Eldem

Sedad Eldem combined in his gardens an uncompromising Modernism — as exemplified in this columned garden space — with traditional Turkish architectural and sculptural forms. Perhaps the greatest Turkish architect of the twentieth century, Eldem arranged the gardens or settings for many of his buildings, most notably in the villas he designed along the shores of the Bosphorus. His aim was to create a specifically Turkish style of architecture and garden design for the twentieth century. His most significant contribution to garden design is his book *Türk Bahçeleri* (1976), an exhaustive survey, through paintings, photographs and measured drawings, of the gardens of the Ottoman Empire. It contains painstaking surveys of many gardens that are now lost, and it is the most important single resource for the study of one the world's great garden heritages.

Kiraç Villa, Tarabya, Istanbul, Turkey, 1965–6. **Sedad Eldem (Sedad Hakki Eldem)**. b Istanbul, Turkey, 1908. d Istanbul, Turkey, 1988.

San Cristobal Luis Barragán

Under the sweltering Mexican sun, the flat expanses of vivid reds, pinks and ochres connect with the deep blues of the water and sky. Rigorous and engaging, this carving of the architecture at the San Cristobal ranch creates a serene and uplifting mental space. One of the most influential architects of the twentieth century, Luis Barragán

called himself primarily a landscape architect. A deeply spiritual man, he remained close to his Mexican roots, working and living there most of his life. He drew the foundation of his art from vernacular Mexican architecture but he also integrated the work of French designer Ferdinand Bac and of Le Corbusier. But most of his

enduring 'lessons' came from chance encounters. He recalls a particular epiphany in Granada: 'Having walked through the darkened Alhambra I suddenly emerged into the serene, silent and solitary Patio of the Myrtles. I had the feeling that it enclosed what a perfect garden no matter its size should enclose: nothing less than the entire universe.'

San Cristobal, Egerstrom Residence and Stables, Los Clubes, Mexico City, Mexico, 1968. **Luis Barragán**. b Guadalajara, Mexico, 1902. d Mexico City, Mexico, 1988.

The Labyrinth Joan Miró

Monumental ceramics on linked terraces people Joan Miró's Labyrinth, among the pines adjacent to the Maeght Foundation building in the French Riviera village of Saint-Paul. It is one of very few examples of an artist creating a series of works for a specific outdoor setting. Miró made full-size plywood models of the sculptures in order to experiment with their positioning. Then his collaborator, the ceramicist Josep Llorens Artigas, helped him realize the final works. Some of the pieces, such as the marble *L'Oiseau Lunaire*, a bird with a horned head, are recognizable figurative subjects; others, such as *Femme à la chevelure défaite*, are abstracts. Miró made eight full-size terracotta models of the largest work, *Le Grand Arc*, before casting it in concrete. At The Labyrinth, Miró fulfilled his ambition to work on a monumental scale in an architectural context. Unusually, the outdoor spaces (by Miró and Alberto Giacometti) and the building were designed simultaneously, to complement each other.

The Labyrinth, Maeght Foundation, Saint-Paul, France, 1963–8. **Joan Miró**. **b** Barcelona, Spain, 1893. **d** Palma de Moyona, Spain, 1983.

Wexham Springs Dame Sylvia Crowe

The concrete blocks used for this textured wall contrast with the smooth-cast concrete floor, steps and sculptural water basin, the whole blending with the more natural materials of water-washed cobbles and plant matter. Dame Sylvia Crowe, a contemporary of Sir Geoffrey Jellicoe and Brenda Colvin, was mainly occupied by large-scale

commissions such as the layout of new towns, nuclear power stations, forestry plantations, reservoirs and the routing of the National Grid. Her landscape designs reflected loyalty to Capability Brown and Humphry Repton, yet she never lost the connection between the garden and its role, as she observed in *Garden Design*, her magnum

opus of 1958: 'Men in every age have felt the need to reconcile themselves with their surroundings, and have created gardens to satisfy their ideals and inspirations.' This ethos is evident in all her gardens. This garden (since demolished) was modern in style, created for the Cement and Concrete Association, and a new-town setting.

Wexham Springs, Wexham, Slough, Buckinghamshire, UK, 1969. **Dame Sylvia Crowe**. **b** Banbury, Oxfordshire, UK, 1901. **d** London, UK, 1997.

Schoten Garden Jacques, Peter & Martin Wirtz

A cloud hedge, an idea derived from Japanese garden design, forms an abstract, undulating relief of boxwood at Jacques Wirtz's own garden in Belgium. With his sons, Peter and Martin, Wirtz creates gardens underpinned by an organic formalism, in which large numbers of suitable plants, such as beech, hornbeam, yew and box, are clipped and shaped to create walls and buttresses to complement sculpture, smooth greensward and reflective expanses of water. In this garden, Wirtz has allowed the established evergreen framework to grow almost unchecked — hence its pleasingly random appearance. Wirtz is also a dedicated horticulturist, and luxuriant borders of perennials and plantations of fruit trees recur in his schemes. In 1998 the Duchess of Northumberland commissioned the Wirtzes to produce designs for a formal water garden in the old walled garden at Alnwick Castle.

Schoten Garden, Schoten, Antwerp, Belgium, from 1970. **Jacques Wirtz**. b Antwerp, Belgium, 1924. **Peter Wirtz**. b Schoten, Antwerp, Belgium, 1961.
Martin Wirtz. b Schoten, Antwerp, Belgium, 1963.

Leitzsch Residence A E Bye

On a woodland site near Ridgefield, in western Connecticut, A E Bye worked his subtle magic, merging and entwining art and nature. The balconies and docks of the house have been built to extend into the surrounding landscape. Vistas have been cut through the woods, pushing the view out into the distance and establishing the garden in a larger setting. Bye liked to juxtapose nature and humanity, bringing the woods right up to the windows of the house. He did not believe in introducing exotic species that would disturb the natural ecology of a site and pose problems of cultivation and maintenance. It worried him to think that the natural character of the local environment might disappear because native species are being replaced by plants from other parts of the world. Bye is also well known for his fieldscapes: undulating turf reminiscent of ancient earthworks.

Leitzsch Residence, nr Ridgefield, CT, USA, mid–late 1970s. **A E Bye (Arthur Edwin Bye)**. **b** Arnhem, The Netherlands, 1919. **d** Doylestown, PA, USA, 2001.

Barbara Hepworth Sculpture Garden Dame Barbara Hepworth

Positioned exactly how and where she wanted it, and taking full advantage of changing shadows and surrounding planting, this sculpture is one of a collection of Dame Barbara Hepworth's works that transforms the small garden adjacent to her Trewyn Studio into an outside gallery. Studying the sculptures in the way that Hepworth wished them to be seen provides an extra insight into the works themselves and the philosophy behind her art. Hepworth was convinced that 'Full sculptural expression is spatial — it is a three-dimensional realization of the idea, either by mass or spatial construction … There must be a perfect unity between the idea, the substance, and the dimension … The idea … actually is the giving of life and vitality to material … Vitality is not a physical, organic attribute … it is spiritual inner life.' This can be seen in the sculptures themselves, but since it is an ethos that applies equally to garden design, the overall experience is greater than the sum of the individual parts.

Barbara Hepworth Museum & Sculpture Garden, St Ives, Cornwall, UK, c1949–75. **Dame Barbara Hepworth**. b Wakefield, Yorkshire, UK, 1903. d St Ives, Cornwall, UK, 1975.

Garden of Rest, Brion-Vega Tomb Carlo Scarpa

This uncompromisingly modern Garden of Rest is enclosed in a sharp, clearly delineated environment, although one can distinguish an underlying narrative and poetical approach that steers it away from arid functionalism. When he designed this private family tomb in the Cemetery of San Vito d'Altivole in 1970, the Italian architect Carlo

Scarpa said he was trying 'to further what meaning there was in death, in the ephemerality of life'. Scarpa is perhaps better known for his many important historical restorations. Being Venetian born and bred may have predisposed him to think in terms of the historic fabric inherent to a place. He had an instinctive gift for combining the existing historic

elements of a site with newly invented ones. He applied this approach successfully in a number of private gardens, as in the courtyard of the Castelvecchio Museum in Verona. The Brion-Vega Tomb was, however, most important to Scarpa, and he asked to be buried there. As he himself liked to say: 'The place for the dead is the garden.'

Garden of Rest, Brion-Vega Tomb, Cemetery of San Vito d'Altivole, Treviso, Italy, 1970–8. **Carlo Scarpa**. b Venice, Italy, 1906. d Sendai, Japan, 1978.

Denmans John Brookes

Denmans is the home of garden designer John Brookes, whose book *Room Outside* (1969) popularized the now-familiar concept of outdoor living and 'patio gardening'. The 14-hectare (3.5-acre) garden lies on stony, alkaline soil close to England's south coast. It was begun by the late Joyce Robinson, who arrived in 1946 and subsequently laid out a 'dry river' of gravel, running in sinuous curves down a gentle slope, planted with silver birch trees and Mediterranean-type plants. Robinson's innovative gravel garden was inspired by a visit she had made to the Greek island of Delos in the late 1960s. When Brookes arrived in 1980 he continued the theme of planting in a stony landscape and also made a fragrant, informal herb garden within the former walled kitchen garden. Now in its maturity, this garden shows a relaxed style, at ease with itself, since its most attractive plants are allowed to self-sow, with pleasing informality.

Denmans, Fontwell, West Sussex, UK, 1980. **John Brookes. b** Durham, UK, 1933.

Uetliberg Garden Dieter Kienast

Separating the beautifully composed gardens from a steep wooded slope, a balustrade spells out 'I too was in Arcadia'. The late Swiss garden designer Dieter Kienast inscribed this much-debated quote relating to Virgil's ideal land into the landscape, thereby constructing a distinctive picturesque image for the end of the twentieth century. But this arcadia, defined by a remarkable blend of nature and pure architecture, is to do with an awareness of our contemporary condition. Sometimes considered a 'minimalist' master due to his voluntarily limited palette of plants and his focus on a few architectural elements, Kienast liked to quote the American minimal artist Robert Morris: 'Simplicity of shape does not equate with simplicity of experience.' In particular, Kienast brought new meaning to the notion of edging: borders, paths, terraces, walls, canals and pools intersect with almost transcendent precision.

Uetliberg Garden, Zürich, Switzerland, c1980. **Dieter Kienast**. **b** Zürich, Switzerland, 1945. **d** London, UK, 1998.

Private Residence Patrick Watson

Massive boulders of burnt-orange granite, sourced locally, define the garden designed by Patrick Watson in a suburb of Johannesburg. The client had an interest in Japanese garden design, hence the koi carp, bamboos, still water and the careful placement of rocks to create a meditative atmosphere. Water surrounds the house, following the contours of the land, and even travels beneath it, through a grotto-like tunnel. The rock fig (*Ficus ingens*) and the small evergreen *Euclea crispa* scramble across the rocks of the terraces that descend from the house. Like other forward-looking designers, Watson avoids the obvious Sissinghurst pastiche traditionally favoured in English-speaking countries, and uses instead the native flora to dramatic effect. In this case his planting includes indigenous bulbs, such as zephyranthes, schizostylis and crinum lilies.

Private Residence, Sandton, Johannesburg, South Africa, c1980. **Patrick Watson**. Active South Africa, twenty-first century.

Private Garden Shodo Suzuki

Asymmetrical and rectilinear, this stone stream occupies most of the space in the garden of a private residence in Chichibu. This assured and superbly simple design plays on almost imperceptible but dramatic changes of levels, with the strong horizontals emphasized further by the flat-topped stones. In this perfectly balanced composition, the placement and treatment of the stones denotes a superior understanding of the material. Combined with water and a few well-chosen plants, they provide the complete, age-old tools of the traditional Japanese garden designer and Shodo Suzuki doesn't feel the need to expand on it in this small garden. Inside these parameters, however, Suzuki conjures up radically new designs, and a whole new language. Widely influential, he designed many public spaces in Japan, sometimes using unexpected materials, but always espousing the same simple techniques and basic aesthetic precepts.

Private Garden, Chichibu, Japan, c1980. **Shodo Suzuki**. Active Japan, twenty-first century.

Safra Bank Roof Garden Roberto Burle Marx

A multi-talented artist — a painter, sculptor, singer, jewellery designer and skilled plantsman with a passion for Brazilian flora (he even discovered several new species) — Roberto Burle Marx is remembered as one of the most important landscape architects of the twentieth century. His first garden dates from 1932 and he established his private practice in 1955. His early works were very influential in inspiring a generation of landscape architects to develop a modern garden form in the yeårs after World War II. This roof garden is like many of Burle Marx's creations inasmuch as that when viewed from above (or in plan) it looks like an enlargement of one of his paintings. Here, plants are subsidiary to the various types of paving stones that take the place of paints. In other compositions, such as the Flamengo Park, the amorphous and sinuous shapes are picked out by mass plantings of vibrant indigenous plants characterized by the striking juxtapositions of bright colours.

Safra Bank Roof Garden, São Paulo, Brazil, 1982. **Roberto Burle Marx**. b São Paulo, Brazil, 1909. d Rio de Janeiro, Brazil, 1994.

Parc de la Villette Bernard Tschumi

One of twenty-five 'follies' in La Villette's vast urban park, this bright red metal structure is, like the other constructions, based on the systematic 'deconstruction' and rearrangement of a 10-m (33-ft) cube. Dotted around the multifunction park in an exact grid at 120-m (394-ft) intervals, they represent the points in an organization where walkways and covered avenues are lines, while lawns and bare earth are surfaces. Architect Bernard Tschumi devised this radical scheme for the revamping of the site of the huge old slaughterhouses east of Paris in the early 1980s. It was chosen after a controversial competition and fuelled a very public but constructive debate on the state of public architecture, urbanism and landscape. Its incorporation of Jacques Derrida's concept of deconstruction in the physical and functional dimensions was revolutionary. One of the first radically postmodern projects ever realized, it also uncompromisingly addressed the idea of a 'cultured' nature.

Parc de la Villette, Paris, France, 1982. Bernard Tschumi. b Lausanne, Switzerland, 1944.

54

Hummelo Piet Oudolf

This view of 'new perennial' plantings in Piet Oudolf's own garden demonstrates exactly why he is such an influential garden designer and nurseryman. Historically he may be seen as reconciling the German traditions of large-scale natural planting promoted by Karl Foerster with the traditional herbaceous borders of the English school, represented by Gertrude Jekyll. In so doing, he enables the owners of small private gardens to combine maximum effect with minimum maintenance. He is a master of mood: he believes light, movement, harmony, control, the sublime and the mystical are all attainable within the garden. His designs combine forms and colours, repetition and rhythm, shrubs and herbaceous plants. Those plants may be structural or infills, natural or contrived: many are grasses and umbellifers, since his plantings give value to form and leaves as much as colour. And he is strongly aware of the changing seasons, and the need for a garden to give pleasure all year round.

Hummelo, Arnhem, The Netherlands, from 1982. **Piet Oudolf (Kwekerij Piet Oudolf)**. b Haarlem, The Netherlands, 1944.

Dickenson Garden Martha Schwartz

The entrance courtyard at the Dickenson Garden in Santa Fe, New Mexico, is a modern update of the geometric Islamic tradition. Four raised brick plinths containing small fountains are connected by brightly coloured, tiled runnels. Nine flowering crab-apple trees embedded in large chunks of white Colorado marble complete the grid-like effect, which is especially effective at night. On the other side of the modern adobe house, views over wide-open desert spaces open up from a terrace. 'It's kind of like a Frank Lloyd Wright thing,' Schwartz explains. 'You create a pressurized space, then you are released by the wider landscape.' Schwartz is one of the most consistently innovative and iconoclastic landscape artists working today. Recent works include the Mesa Arts Center in Arizona and the Grand Canal Square in Dublin, Ireland, but her most famous work is probably the 1979 Bagel Garden, for which Schwartz adorned her own tiny Boston front yard with real varnished bagels.

Dickenson Garden, Santa Fe, NM, USA, 1982. **Martha Schwartz. b** Philadelphia, PA, USA, 1950.

Douglas Garden Steve Martino

A small house sits in the Arizona desert, surrounded by the sculptural verticals of the scrub-covered hills and the indigenous saguro cactus. Steve Martino is one of the leading landscape architects and designers in the American south-west. He became known during the 1980s and 1990s for his work with architects on the siting of new houses in the context of the desert environment. He is also respected for his broad and deep knowledge of desert plant subjects and their uses in the landscape. Many of his garden and landscape designs flow seamlessly from the areas around a private house or public building into the surrounding desert. The plants Martino uses are chosen for their innate sculptural qualities. Even though he works primarily in a single region, he is not unaware of leading designers of the twentieth century; Alvar Aalto is a considerable influence.

Douglas Garden, Phoenix, AZ, USA, 1982. **Steve Martino**. b Phoenix, AZ, USA, 1946.

The Valentine House Isabelle Greene

Spiky agaves, grasses, aloes and yuccas punctuate a patchwork of low-growing succulent plants in a garden designed to be viewed as much from above as from within. Isabelle Greene responded to the Modernist pueblo house by softening the hard edges with bougainvillea and espaliered figs. The view from the first-floor terrace was inspired by views of agricultural land from the air, and the areas with succulents (among them green cerastium, blue kleinia, reddish sedum, pink kalanchoe) are designed to resemble field patterns. The terraces are formed by terracotta-coloured concrete cast in cedarwood moulds. From the bottom of the garden looking back to the house, their horizontal alignment creates a sense of foreshortened distance, another deliberate effect. Greene has had a garden-design practice in California since the early 1960s, and she has received most of her commissioned work from within the state.

The Valentine House, Santa Barbara, CA, USA, 1985. **Isabelle Greene. b** USA, 1934.

The Red Garden Jack Lenor Larsen

Parallel rows of rough cedar trunks, painted in the blazing red of Japanese Shinto gates and interplanted with scarlet azaleas, contrast with the complementary greens of the grass and higher-level planting to produce a vista of almost shocking intensity. This piece of modern garden sculpture is the work of Jack Lenor Larsen, who for over fifty years has been one of the world's leading textile designers. The 'Larsen Look' has evolved to become synonymous with modern sophistication. Construction of the house and garden began in 1986, and at the end of 1991 Larsen established the LongHouse Foundation (later Reserve), which aims to demonstrate a way of living with art and to create landscapes as an art form. The result is a garden of immense vitality and variety, where locally inspired features are combined with references to far-off places, such as an amphitheatre based on ancient Irish ring forts. Found or recycled objects (like the cedar posts) sit alongside commissioned pieces, and old is juxtaposed with new.

The Red Garden, Longhouse Reserve, East Hampton, NY, USA, 1986. **Jack Lenor Larsen**. b Seattle, WA, USA, 1927.

Sutton Place Sir Geoffrey Jellicoe

A much-enlarged version of a relief sculpture by Ben Nicholson, surrounded by yew hedges and prefaced by a rectangular pond, is the endpiece of Geoffrey Jellicoe's major (albeit unfinished) work, the garden at Sutton Place commissioned by Stanley Seeger in 1980. Jellicoe's intention was to make a Modernist garden of distinct features that were intended to be visited in a specific order. The programme is based on man's passage through life, from birth to death, and is informed by Jellicoe's preoccupation with the philosophy of Carl Jung. Birth is represented by a huge lake in the shape of a foetus; death and beyond by the Nicholson wall. Surviving features at Sutton Place include a Surrealist walk — a homage to Magritte, with huge urns that create an optical illusion — and the Paradise Garden, a delightful space of meandering paths, fountains and rose arbours. Jellicoe was an architect who turned to landscape after a tour of Italian Renaissance gardens in the 1920s.

Sutton Place, Sutton Park, Sutton Green, Guildford, Surrey, UK, 1980–6. **Sir Geoffrey Jellicoe**. b London, UK, 1900. d Seaton, Devon, UK, 1996.

Meyer Garden Wolfgang Oehme & James van Sweden

A path winds through bold masses of grasses and bright perennials. Swaying in the wind, the plants seem to owe nothing to human hand and look as if they had always grown right there on each side of this natural looking path. This seamless planting and deceptively simple design are the trade mark of James van Sweden and Wolfgang

Oehme, who in the early 1990s were credited with the invention of the 'New American Garden'. This now-familiar image of a loose and free garden planted with simple, often native, perennials and, most importantly, grasses, was a novelty in 1990. Unlike many of his contemporaries, van Sweden didn't believe in remodelling the landscape,

preferring to go along with the existing topography. He also rejected the use of lawns, which he calls 'green concrete', and clipped evergreens. Instead, with the help of his botanist partner Oehme, he wanted to put the focus back on plants that change according to the seasons, harmonizing and composing natural schemes.

Meyer Garden, Harbert, MI, USA, 1989. **Wolfgang Oehme**. b Chemnitz, Germany, 1930. **James van Sweden**. b Grand Rapids, MI, USA, 1935.

Schnabel House Frank Gehry

A path of Californian sandstone leads past a seemingly haphazard grouping of metallic shapes, which form the office, to the series of boxes that make up the living area. This is architect Frank Gehry's essay in suburban deconstructivism, in which the components of a house are taken apart and rearranged to make a sculpture garden in which to live. The house was built between 1987 and 1989 in the wealthy Brentwood district of California, with landscaping by Nancy Goslee Power. The separation of living spaces produced a variety of outdoor areas, thus extending the perceived size of the 2,320 sq m (25,000 sq ft) plot. The largely drought-tolerant plants are cleverly used in conjunction with the architecture. For example, the radially branching palms, phormiums and cordylines make a striking counterpoint to the angular buildings, while the olive grove adds a softening, rural feel to the harsh modern setting.

Schnabel House, Brentwood, CA, USA, 1987–9. **Frank Owen Gehry. b** Toronto, ON, Canada, 1929.

Mien Ruys Tuinen Mien Ruys

Mien Ruys began her career by designing borders for the landscaping section of her father's nursery business at Moerheimstraat, Dedemsvaart. She began to lay out small model gardens there in 1925, beginning with the Wild Garden and the old Experimental Garden with the pebbled concrete slabs that she designed and which are now commonplace. By 1929 Ruys was studying garden architecture seriously and later joined a group of progressive architects who believed in functionalism. This was followed by a period of teaching landscape architecture. It was twenty-five years before she again began to add to the gardens at Dedemsvaart, with the Water Garden in 1954, pictured here, and the Herb Garden in 1957. She experimented with new plants and materials such as the innovative use of railway sleepers and recycled plastics. The twenty-five gardens at Mien Ruys Tuinen are a permanent record of her design ideas.

Mien Ruys Tuinen, Dedemsvaart, The Netherlands, 1925–90. Mien Ruys. b Dedemsvaart, The Netherlands, 1904. d Deventer, The Netherlands, 1999.

'Taking a Wall for a Walk' Andy Goldsworthy

This structure in Grizedale Forest is a snaking serpentine wall. It was made by Andy Goldsworthy, an artist and sculptor well known for creating either temporary or permanent outdoor structures from natural materials that he has collected locally. These might be leaves, the branches of trees, pebbles or snow. At Grizedale Forest — the 17.5-sq-km (7-sq-mile) plantation forest and leisure park in England's Lake District — he has drawn inspiration from the local vernacular of dry stone walling. This serpentine section, built by a team of skilled wallers, weaves like a sidewinder rattlesnake through the larches and firs for around 137 m (450 ft). It has embraced, rather than flattened, any trees in its path. The forest itself contains a network of old stone walls, dating from when the area was open pasture. Goldsworthy, who relishes the functional nature of stone walls, manipulated the traditional straight-lined wall 'to articulate a changing relationship between people and place'.

'Taking a Wall for a Walk', Grizedale Forest Park, Ambleside, Cumbria, UK, 1990. **Andy Goldsworthy**. b Cheshire, UK, 1956.

Miguel Gomez Residence José de Yturbe

The bright walls of this spectacular courtyard, in which slots in the walls act as windows, defining the view out over the tropical hills beyond and letting in natural sunlight, are in contrast with the striking patio of recinto (black volcanic rock chips) and marble, and the fountain made out of carved volcanic rock. This is typical of José de Yturbe's work, in which he reinterprets Mexican vernacular architecture. He has also been strongly influenced by the work of the Mexican architect Luis Barragán, and his courtyards, where he tries to establish the notion of dwelling rather than building by allowing plants to invade the architecture, clearly reveal both inspiration sources.

His designs show an intimacy, privacy and serenity, which is enhanced by the acoustic effects of moving water. The use of water reflects the strong Islamic influences in the Iberian peninsula, a legacy of the Moorish conquest. De Yturbe's use of strong colour also has echoes of the work of the painter Jesús Reyes Ferreira.

Miguel Gomez Residence, San José, Costa Rica, c1990. **José de Yturbe**. b Mexico City, Mexico, 1942.

Show Case House Madison Cox

Terracotta pots of foxgloves are playfully arranged on a chequer-board of gravel in this Manhattan rooftop garden, the strong framework echoing the grid of the city below. This is a town garden par excellence. The garden is not designed to be used, and the very graphic layout is all for show — Madison Cox prefers his gardens to have a sharp

structure. Clear definition and strict organization are, in his eyes, the best way to achieve a peaceful environment. Though he is a keen plantsman, Cox puts little emphasis on plants, preferring to use a relatively narrow repertory of evergreen shrubs, vines and trees to soften and dress his strong structures. Having chosen to train in France,

this New Yorker established himself in Paris, where he designed elegant town gardens for private *hôtels particuliers* and public spaces like the Franco-American Museum. He eventually returned to his bustling home town to create rooftop oases.

Show Case House, New York, NY, USA, 1990s. **Madison Cox. b** Washington, DC, USA, 1958.

University Botanic Garden Ivar Otruba

The Botanic Garden of the University of Brno is one of the most significant twentieth-century gardens in Central Europe. Its designer, Ivar Otruba, derives his inspiration not from any previous or contemporary garden style, but from his own unique imagination. His style is based on a set of natural features — prairies, mountain torrents and a mountainside — the latter forming an appropriate location for the garden's collection of alpine plants. In this, vertical dividers of concrete or sheet metal separate natural rock compositions representing different mountain formations and their plants. In another area, lumps of tufa rock raised to eye-level on metal poles support miniature alpine gardens. Otruba's creation is highly unusual — if not unique — as a large botanic garden that is characterized by an original and consistent design style. William Chambers's original plan for Kew fitted this description, but little of it remains.

University Botanic Garden, Mendel University of Agriculture & Forestry, Brno, Czech Republic, 1990s. **Ivar Otruba**. b Czech Republic, 1933.

Stockholm Residence Ulf Nordfjell

Massed plantings of sedums offset the uncompromising Modernist monolith of a house at this private residence near Stockholm. Since the birth of Modernism, garden designers have struggled to find a design vocabulary that complements this style of architecture. Ulf Nordfjell's planting design at this property typifies the approach advocated in recent years of massed, informal plantings of perennials and grasses that sway in the wind and contrast with the smooth, immutable planes of the architecture. In Nordfjell's work craggy boulders, slabs of stone and gravel are carefully placed to echo the natural landscape of Sweden, and this harshness is offset by sophisticated planting schemes incorporating herbaceous perennials that will survive the winters. Nordfjell is also an accomplished ceramicist, and a high standard of decoration characterizes his work.

Stockholm Residence, Stockholm, Sweden, 1990s. **Ulf Nordfjell. b** Umeå, Sweden, 1948.

Wheat Garden Fernando Caruncho

Inscribed into this Spanish landscape, following the grid of orange groves and plough marks, this garden shows a high degree of formality, albeit expressed in a contemporary fashion. Although it never attempts to mimic an ancient pattern, it could have been there since time immemorial, belonging to an undiscovered civilization. Fernando Caruncho is undoubtedly heir to the Spanish garden tradition, which is rooted in the Moorish style and the Alhambra at Granada. He is also a great admirer of such gardens as Vaux-le-Vicomte near Paris and the Boboli in Florence. But his particular brand of formality runs deep; it is not a simple design tool but a fundamental belief, inspired by his philosophical studies, notably of the Ancient Greeks. The sense of order and balance, of permanence and history, is achieved by bringing together Caruncho's own aesthetic heritage and the history of the landscape. He is particularly interested in the science of irrigation and ancient agricultural patterns.

Wheat Garden, Palma de Mallorca, Spain, 1991. **Fernando Caruncho (Fernando Caruncho Torga)**. b Madrid, Spain, 1957.

Smith Residence Vladimir Sitta

Black bamboo (*Phyllostachys nigra*) and tufts of mondo grass border a simple rectangular pool that culminates in a relief sculpture. At this private Sydney garden, Vladimir Sitta has created a formal space with a strong Japanese tone. Sitta has emerged over the last decade as one of the leading avant-garde designers currently working in Australia. His work often incorporates geologically inspired elements, such as fissures cracking through otherwise pristine stone, artificial mist and monolithic slabs. In the Smith Residence garden, two jagged spears of stone bisect the reflections of the pool and lend it an elemental quality that compromises what would otherwise be an example of pristine Modernism. In the best Japanese tradition, Sitta explores this tension between order and untamed nature. Sitta's garden designs are among the most closely followed for their originality.

Smith Residence, Sydney, NSW, Australia, 1991. **Vladimir Sitta. b** Czech Republic, 1954.

Parc André Citroën Gilles Clément & Alain Provost

A series of rectangular ramped lawns of varying widths give a slightly lopsided symmetry to this vista at Parc André Citroën in Paris. The scattering of informally planted Versailles tubs adds another playful twist to classic design tradition. On the former site of the Citroën car works, the celebrated French landscape designers Gilles Clément and Alain Provost have created a public space of dazzling inventiveness. The various themed areas include Black, White and Blue Gardens, Six Sense Gardens and a plaza where children run through random water jets. Although it deliberately echoes the formal layout of other great Parisian parks, Parc André Citroën makes a distinctly contemporary appeal to mind, body and spirit, as well as complementing the surrounding modern architecture. Provost is responsible for the Great Lawn to the right of the photograph, while Clément — who famously hates lawns — designed the Garden of Movement, a meadow where plants move in the breeze.

Parc André Citroën, Paris, France, 1986–92. **Gilles Clément**. b Argenton-sur-Creuse, Indre, France, 1943. **Alain Provost**. b France, 1938.

Golders Green Garden Paul Cooper

A projection of Roy Lichtenstein's iconic Pop Art piece *Wham!* enlivens the night-time ambience of a small north London garden. The garden's owners intended to use the garden mainly at night, so Paul Cooper incorporated smooth white panels into his design to provide the potential for constantly changing visuals in this enclosed space.

Architectural and textile designs are particularly effective projections. Metal balustrades section off small areas of the decked terrace, and a selection of shrubs grown for their foliage effects (hebes, bamboos, euphorbias) are confined to raised planters. A stainless-steel cascade — cleverly lit — adds to the nocturnal drama. Cooper is an

iconoclastic figure in contemporary garden design, well known for showcasing outrageous ideas, such as floating planters or mid-air hanging baskets, at Chelsea Flower Show. On one occasion he was censured for incorporating erotic drawings in his design.

Golders Green Garden, London, UK, 1992, renovated 2001. **Paul Cooper. b** Manchester, UK, 1949.

Les Buissons Optiques Bernard Lassus

In this show garden, the extraordinary combinations of colours, textures and planes were based on careful optical and mathematical observations. They reflect Bernard Lassus's preoccupation with the interplay between imaginary space and what he calls 'real space'. Another important consideration in Lassus's thought processes are the layered references to the various levels of history and culture. Having trained with Fernand Léger, Lassus has long expressed himself through conceptual art. Today he is highly respected as a landscape architect and designer, as well as theoretician and teacher. He has realized such prestigious projects as the Jardins des Retours in Rochefort and worked on huge portions of the French motorway system. But Lassus has also lost important competitions — the restoration of the Tuileries for example. He has however recently completed the highly acclaimed Hanging Gardens of Colas for the corporate company in Boulogne-Billancourt, France.

Les Buissons Optiques, Niort, France, 1993. **Bernard Lassus. b** Chamalières, France, 1929.

IBM Solana Peter Walker

An *allée* of poplars encloses a dead-straight canal at one of Peter Walker's biggest commissions, an IBM office complex, hotel and 'village' in Texas. Walker is the leading contemporary proponent of large-scale formalism and, like Le Nôtre before him, he sculpts with space as if it were a physical entity. A variety of formal, modern effects embellishes IBM Solana: *allées* of trees, parterres, viewing benches, sculptural features such as a vast circular stone mound emanating mist and, within the complex, intimate formal courtyard gardens. The furthest reaches of the 340-hectare (850-acre) site have been planted with prairie, wild-flower meadows and new-oak woodland. Walker's use of repeated or subtly varied motifs on a large scale, and his ability to create startling new features as a focus, have improved public spaces in the USA and Japan, notably the Center for Advanced Science and Technology in Hyogo, the Toyota Municipal Museum of Art, Japan, and the plaza at Costa Mesa, California.

IBM Solana, Solana, TX, USA, 1984–93. **Peter Walker**. b USA, 1932.

Garden of Fine Arts Tadao Ando

Lying on the base of a long pool, Claude Monet's *Waterlilies* shimmer under a shallow layer of clear water. All around, the concrete lines of the walls, large panes of glass and sheets of flowing water carve up the sky and delineate the space. Further on are more reproductions of some of art history's most revered masterpieces (Leonardo da Vinci's *Last Supper*, Georges Seurat's *La Grande Jatte* and so on) providing sources of colour and texture in this dramatic open-air structure of concrete and water. Highly durable, these life-size reproductions are photographs transposed and fired on to ceramic panels. Tadao Ando is one of the most influential architects of the late twentieth century. In this garden he has applied the architectural theories that are so beautifully expressed in his churches and temples. Ando is a self-taught, widely travelled figure with a highly independent attitude to building. Zen philosophy and traditional Japanese architecture inform his constant concern with landscape and the elements.

Garden of Fine Arts, Kyoto National Museum, Kyoto, Japan, 1994. **Tadao Ando**. **b** Osaka, Japan, 1941.

Mur Végétal Patrick Blanc

Growing on a near vertical wall, an attractive group of plants thrives as if in a perennial border. At first glance, the Mur Végétal is a mystery. It is as beautiful as a natural cliff covered in flowers and vegetation. A small pool below — home to a few goldfish — collects continuously trickling water. The wall itself consists of a fine wire mesh stretched on a metal structure which is covered in a thick layer of felt. With no earth involved here, the vegetation is 'planted' in pockets of the felt fabric. It germinates and grows thanks only to the presence of water. Despite its highly attractive appearance, this was a significant scientific experiment undertaken by the French agronomist Patrick Blanc at the annual garden festival of Chaumont-sur-Loire in 1994. It has now become a permanent installation there and the technique is being perfected, finding practical applications in various French cities.

Mur Végétal, International Garden Festival, Château de Chaumont-sur-Loire, nr Tours, France, 1994. **Patrick Blanc**, b Paris, France, 1953.

VSB Bank Adriaan Geuze

An elegant footbridge spans the breadth of this linear garden, where long blocks of low box hedges alternate with bands of red stone chippings. Stretching out along the curve of the painted metal bridge, a wooden bench invites quiet contemplation of this corporate garden, created in 1994 by the Dutch designer Adriaan Geuze, a leading light of the West 8 landscape group. He has worked on projects ranging from huge dammed areas on the North Sea to Schiphol Airport. Describing himself as a functionalist and a 'hyperrealist', Geuze doesn't believe in creating idealistic and supposedly soothing green spaces at this time in our history. He believes in taking full account of contemporary realities, such as increased speed or restricted space, and using the materials that constitute our environment — such as steel, asphalt or concrete. This positive reclamation of the environment is evolved from constant confrontation with the intensely man-altered landscape of his native Holland.

VSB Bank, Utrecht, The Netherlands, 1994. **Adriaan Geuze**. b Dordrecht, The Netherlands, 1960.

Prospect Cottage Derek Jarman

Derek Jarman's unique, totemic sculptures, made of pebbles and flotsam, and his exuberant and unlikely plantings, surround a small, wooden, fisherman's cottage on an exposed pebble beach in Kent, in the shadow of the Dungeness B nuclear power station. The garden rapidly became (and still is) a cult destination, inspiring many imitations, most of them poor. 'I invest my stones with the power of Avebury,' Jarman wrote. 'I have read all the mystical books about leylines and circles — I built the circles with this behind my mind.' In the unearthly and beautiful landscape of Dungeness, Jarman's sculptures of driftwood, rusted metal and weathered stones took on a magical quality. The success of his gardening was equally arresting, with bright poppies, marigolds, irises and dog roses thriving next to the less surprising sea kale, santolina and cotton lavender. The garden survives.

Prospect Cottage, Dungeness, Kent, UK, 1987–94. **Derek Jarman**, b Pinner Hill, Middlesex, UK, 1942. d London, UK, 1994.

Site of Reversible Destiny Arakawa & Gins

In a vast oval bowl that sits in the landscape like a geological accident, a world of small hills, bizarre constructions and wonky paths on uneven ground awaits the visitor. The Site of Reversible Destiny in Kyoto is meant to overturn one's perceptions and destabilize physically and conceptually — only to eventually 'open a new

horizon'. Here, as in a traditional Japanese stroll garden, on each turn one will encounter a new vista: ranges of half-sunken kitchen units colliding with upturned sofas, flat staircases or tiled roofs on the floor. Japanese-born conceptual artist Shushaku Arakawa, now based in New York with his American partner, writer and artist Madeline

Gins, has been given the opportunity to take the concept of deconstruction on to a new plane. Using the traditional garden device of the labyrinth in a series of physical encounters, they add a textual layer with a set of 'Directions for Use' in a leaflet distributed to each visitor.

Site of Reversible Destiny, Yoro Park, Kyoto, Japan, 1995. **Arakawa & Gins**. **Shushaku Arakawa**. b Nagoya, Japan, 1936. **Madeline Gins**. b New York, NY, USA, 1941.

Grande Isle Pathway Susan Child

Zigzagging through beech and birch woodland towards a meadow, a raised wooden boardwalk path ends as abruptly as it begins. Elsewhere on this huge 32.3-hectare (80-acre) site overlooking Lake Champlain in Vermont, stairs, viewing platforms, a rustic pavilion and other raised pathways are used to draw attention to the special character of the landscape. With this minimal intervention by Susan Child, the lake's shore, the woodlands, the lowlands and the meadows are left undisturbed. It is the visitor's perception that changes and becomes heightened. Walkers are encouraged to explore their own feelings as well as the landscape: standing to contemplate the view on a platform, walking between the sections of boardwalk, sitting in meditation in the pavilion. With her practice based in Boston, Child has produced some of her finer works in New England, undoubtedly inspired by the landscape. Her most famous work, however, is the landscaping of the South Cove in Manhattan's Battery Park (1990s).

Grande Isle Pathway, Grande Isle, VT, USA, 1995. **Susan Child**. b USA, 1928.

Plastic Garden Dean Cardasis

Coloured Plexiglas panels create a remarkable formal division in this now-vanished but widely noted garden design. The idea for a plastic garden sprang from Dean Cardasis's view that the vinyl-sided suburban house, part of a new development, looked like a plastic toy simply thrown onto the landscape. Red and yellow plastic panels form the perimeter to a gravelled outdoor room, while blue panels are used to roof part of the decked area adjoining the house. A sense of enclosure is created through the planting of native trees at the edges of the garden, designed to enmesh eventually with the mature forest beyond, which was cut back by the developers. The garden was relatively cheap to make and was designed as a low-maintenance space with the safety and inspiration of children's play in mind. Cardasis is a professor in landscape architecture at the University of Massachusetts and also a practising designer.

Plastic Garden, Northampton, MA, USA, 1995. **Dean Cardasis**. b New York, NY, USA, 1949.

Future Garden Newton & Helen Mayer Harrison

The rooftop of The Art and Exhibition Hall of the Federal Republic of Germany hosts a wild meadow interspersed with blue conical towers. The meadow, which forms a 'representational sculpture, a continuously changing, living, colour field' was transplanted from the hilly region of the Eifel where it was threatened by a housing development.

A dry meadow, a wet meadow and a stone meadow were added to it by the ecological artists Helen Mayer Harrison and Newton Harrison in 1996. With this installation they wanted to evoke the healing powers of the European meadow, which they consider the most successful collaborative venture between humans and the rest of

the eco-system. Having shaped our environment over the centuries, the meadow habitat is now endangered by monoculture, overgrazing and overcutting. The Harrisons have worked all over the world to draw attention to the planet's most painful ecological wounds.

Future Garden, The Art and Exhibition Hall of the Federal Republic of Germany, Bonn, Germany, 1996. **Newton Harrison**. b New York, NY, USA, 1932.
Helen Mayer Harrison. b New York, NY, USA, 1929.

Sanders Garden Ted Smyth

A swimming pool with jagged geometric edges, focused on a stainless-steel tubular sculpture, complements a pure white 1980s Modernist house in this New Zealand garden. The smooth, elegant curve of the retaining wall beyond, hemming in a range of subtropical plants (cycads, aloes, dragon trees) produces a satisfying contrast in what is a wide, shallow garden. The designer, Ted Smyth, is little known outside New Zealand, and professes no interest in the design scene. He has created a tranquil space using stainless steel, marble, stone and large-leaved plants. 'I like the anonymity and modernity of materials,' Smyth explains. 'They shouldn't be too animated like terracotta, brass or gold, which are like busy, noisy animals. In order to create serenity and spatial quality you have to reduce the personality of the materials.' At night the garden is lit in eerie blue light, creating reflections in the still pool.

Sanders Garden, Auckland, New Zealand, 1996. **Ted Smyth**. b Auckland, New Zealand, 1937.

Ellison Residence Ron Herman

A three-dimensional chequerboard of black riverwash stones and mind-your-own-business moss (*Soleirolia soleirolii*), overshadowed by bamboos planted in dwarf mondo grass, distinguishes the courtyard at the Ellison Residence. Ron Herman's design for the central courtyard, which can be seen from several rooms inside William Wurster's 1961 Modernist house overlooking San Francisco Bay, was inspired by gardens in Kyoto. Elsewhere at the Ellison Residence Herman has introduced a sleek, brimful rectangular pool, abutted at a right angle by a wall made of opaque, textured blocks of glass overlaid with shiny steel bars. This construction owes something to the later work of the artist Piet Mondrian. The use of barriers — the glass screen, dividing walls, bamboos — helps create a sense of surprise in a relatively small space. Herman's work represents a fusion of Californian Modernism and Japanese Zen precepts.

Ellison Residence, San Francisco, CA, USA, 1997. **Ron Herman. b** Los Angeles, CA, USA, 1941.

The Latin Garden Christopher Bradley-Hole

This 'Virgilian' garden comprised sleek rendered walls, stainless steel, glass panels, contemporary furniture and a bold axis along the whole length of the plot. Quotations from the *Eclogues* were inscribed on stone plaques, a device borrowed from Ian Hamilton Finlay's Little Sparta. London's annual Chelsea Flower Show is not known as a fount of design innovation, but in 1997 Christopher Bradley-Hole's winning show garden, sponsored by the *Daily Telegraph*, marked a stylistic turning point — away from the pastiche of Arts and Crafts, which had reigned supreme for decades. Bradley-Hole is an uncompromising Modernist. The planting utilized a pared-down but effective palette of striking specimens: tall irises and drumstick alliums provided dramatic purple notes above an underplanting of grasses. His example led to a vogue for classical-contemporary show gardens at Chelsea, although the judging panel's need for horticultural sophistication still militates against many contemporary design approaches.

The Latin Garden, Chelsea Flower Show, London, UK, 1997. **Christopher Bradley-Hole. b** Sussex, UK, 1955.

The Tarot Garden Niki de Saint Phalle

Glistening in the Tuscan sun on top of a hill near the Argentario coast, the huge sculptures of the Tarot Garden can be seen for miles around. Covered in bright mosaics, coloured glass or pieces of mirror, they depict various figures in the deck of the 'Sacred Game', forming a mythical and esoteric landscape. The sculptor Niki de Saint Phalle describes a dream she had: while walking in an enchanted garden, she met a multitude of benevolent and magical figures, gigantic and covered in precious stones. Years later she brought her dream to life, giving birth to this highly personal garden of the mind. The widow of Swiss sculptor Jean Tinguely, she scandalized the art world in the 1970s with her giant 'Nanas', her monumental sculptures of women whose brightly coloured bodies could be entered through a door between their spread legs. She worked on the Tarot Garden for twenty years and for some time lived inside the enormous Empress sculpture.

The Tarot Garden, Capalbio, Tuscany, Italy, 1978 98. **Niki de Saint Phalle**. b Neuilly-sur-Seine, France, 1930. d San Diego, CA, USA, 2002.

Fog Garden Peter Latz

Mysterious artificial fog swirls among stone slabs assembled as a twentieth-century henge for the International Garden Festival, Château de Chaumont-sur-Loire, near Tours in France. Artificial fog began to be used by garden and landscape designers twenty years ago. Made by water atomized under high pressure, it was first developed for high-budget public landscape and garden design projects and this is still its prime use. Its time in the private garden has yet to come. The wonderful, mysterious effect blurs landscape elements and boundaries instantly, lending a surreal other-worldliness to the design. Man-made fog has also been used in extremely hot climates for its immediate, but short-term cooling properties. Peter Latz, one of the leading German landscape architects, masterminded the giant post-industrial people's park in the former Thyssen steel works at Duisburg in the Ruhr.

Fog Garden, International Garden Festival, Château de Chaumont-sur-Loire, nr Tours, France, 1997–8. **Peter Latz**. b Darmstadt, Germany, 1939.

'Puffing Mosses' Julie Toll

Moss-covered boulders in a pond belch out white mist to create a slightly disturbing, sci-fi ambience in a Stockholm show garden. Artificial mist has become popular among landscape architects, but usually in a Modernist setting. Toll is unusual in that she brings a modern sensibility to ecological or naturalistic gardening (she dislikes the word 'wild' because it implies a lack of control), here in collaboration with two young Swedish artists, Thomas Nordström and Annika Oskarsson, who constructed the balls of chickenwire, compost and moss, linked by pipes to a mist machine. Toll admits that her work is sometimes more habitat reclamation than design. The native flora is always used as a basis. Working from a base in East Anglia, Toll leads the way in wildflower meadow gardening, a significant contemporary trend. However, unlike contemporaries in the New Perennial movement (Oudolf and Noël Kingsbury, for example), Toll's aim is to produce apparently artless designs taken straight from nature.

'Puffing Mosses', Stockholm, Sweden, 1998. **Julie Toll**. **b** Stourport-on-Severn, Worcestershire, UK, 1953.

Private Garden Tori Winkler Thomas

All gardens are temporary, or at least constantly changing. Some garden spaces, such as this extraordinary vision by Tori Winkler Thomas, exploit this quality to the full, and are expressly made as temporary outdoor installations that survive principally as photographs of one specially constructed moment. Richard Long's sculptures and

Chris Parsons's dew gardens work in a similar way, as did, for example, the diversions within the *bosquets* at Versailles during Louis XIV's nocturnal *fêtes champêtres*. Here, paint has converted plants into living sculpture and the introduction of the white horse lifts the scene to a surreal plane. The *allée* of coloured plants is a prelude to the

gateway that takes the visitor from what is a man-made display into the beauties of naturally planted woodlands. Fallen leaves make an ephemeral pathway to artfully link both aspects of this design. The use of gaudy colours and unusual forms brings a sense of the contemporary to what appears to be an established landscape.

Private Garden, Alexandria, VA, USA, c1998. **Tori Winkler Thomas**. Active USA, twenty-first century.

Glass Garden Andy Cao

Impressionistic swathes of colour are blended together with great subtlety and finesse in Andy Cao's Glass Garden at Echo Park, Los Angeles. The white mounds half-submerged in a blue-lined pool are evocations of the roadside salt mounds Cao remembers from his childhood in Vietnam, and other aspects of the garden — such as

the tufts of the grass *Stipa tenuissima* (redolent of lemon grass) — are also evocations of his native country. Cao started using glass as a material in 1994, after picking up a batch of tumbled table-glass shards from a local recycling depot. He began experimenting with its potential and found that it could be put to many uses in garden

design. The glass, which is safe to walk on barefoot, also acts as a mulch as it suppresses weeds and slows the evaporation of water. Cao has received commissions for more glass-garden designs and has created installations for hotels in Los Angeles and Las Vegas.

Glass Garden. Echo Park, Los Angeles, CA, USA, 1998. **Andy Cao. b** Tây Ninh, Vietnam, 1965.

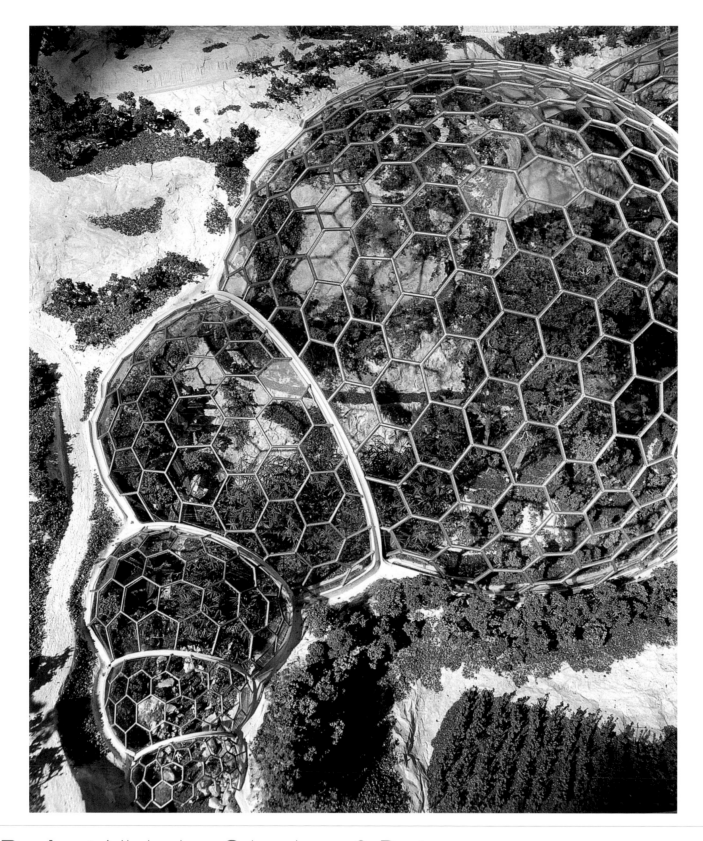

Eden Project Nicholas Grimshaw & Partners

These biomes are the focal point of a visitor attraction and educational project built in a disused china clay pit in Cornwall. The 14-hectare (34.5-acre) bowl-shaped site is 60 m (192 ft) deep with steep, south-facing walls that catch the sun. The biomes are giant conservatories, manufactured with the latest technology and materials and designed to be as energy-efficient as possible. Inside them, two of the world's climate zones have been recreated: the humid tropics (rainforests and Oceania) and the warm temperate regions (the Mediterranean, South African Cape and California). The biomes are alive with plants native to these regions to create a natural and sustainable eco-system. Another, roofless, biome is the temperate zone, and the planting reflects the huge range of native British and exotic plants that thrive in the mild climate of Cornwall.

Eden Project, Bodelva, St Austell, Cornwall, UK, 2001. **Nicholas Grimshaw & Partners**. **Nicholas Grimshaw**. b Hove, East Sussex, UK, 1939.

Villa Kirana Made Wijaya

An Australian, Made Wijaya (born Michael White) is renowned as a tropical garden designer with an excess of 600 gardens to his credit in a range of locations including Mexico, Hawaii, India, Singapore, and of course, Bali. Wijaya first arrived on the island in 1973 and, falling under the spell of the island's culture and architecture, he remained, studied and turned to garden design. Villa Kirana is a private rental villa built near the town of Ubud in a style inspired by a mix of Malay, Balinese Balé and Dutch colonial. Wijaya takes full advantage of the views out over the natural beauty of the Ayung river gorge and Bali's major volcano range, and the man-made terraced landscape of verdant rice fields. His design has no visual boundary and one's eye is carried across to the borrowed landscape beyond, thus making it an intrinsic part of the garden's character.

Villa Kirana, Sayan, Ubud, Bali, 2001. **Made Wijaya (Michael Richard White)**. b Melbourne, VIC, Australia, 1953.

Sustainability Gardens at Turtle Bay Ron Lutsko Jr

Ron Lutsko Jr trained as a horticulturist and landscape architect, and is principal of his own San Francisco-based practice. One of his central spheres of interests is how the form and function of a constructed landscape can be designed in such a way as to simultaneously service the needs of the user, the plantscape and the ecological context of the scheme. Lutsko calls this approach 'sustainable design' and the ethos is a combination of a Modernist approach that incorporates 'regionally appropriate materials in an architecturally refined manner, and presents clear intention for circulation, occupation and interpretation.' The Sustainability Gardens are a public recreational space with the dual purpose of engaging and educating visitors in the complexities of local ecological systems and man's role within them. With its rill, a sinuous stream-like water course, surrounded by stone paving, the design takes full account of local environmental conditions and is constructed using native plants and materials.

Sustainability Gardens at Turtle Bay, Redding, CA, USA, 2003. **Ron Lutsko Jr. b** Oceanside, CA, USA, 1952.

Split Tony Heywood

Educated as an archaeologist and anthropologist, Tony Heywood now describes himself neither as a garden designer nor a sculptor, but a horticultural installation artist. He is known for producing installations ranging in size from the small — for example, 'micro-landscapes' cultivated in a petri dish — to grandiose schemes that cover extensive areas. Site-specific and utilizing unorthodox materials often in allegorical ways, Heywood's works are at the cutting edge of conceptual garden art. Created for the International Festival of the Garden at Westonbirt, Split is typical of his style. Featuring two reflective, modular 'flat pack' monoliths with planting pockets, this unorthodox garden is set within undulating mounds of sward, separated by a valley of stone. In his own words, Heywood's approach is an 'attempt to cross-fertilize the areas of garden design and fine art' using both 'plant and inert matter'. As such, his works are 'pure spectacle and … not functional … not to be entered and should be seen as contemplative works'.

Split, International Festival of the Garden, Westonbirt, The National Arboretum, Tetbury, Gloucestershire, UK, 2003. **Tony Heywood**. Active UK, twenty-first century.   94

Hofu City Crematorium Shunmyo Masuno

Shunmyo Masuno is not only founder and president of his own landscape architecture practice and a professor at Tama Art University, he is also head priest of the Zen Buddhist Kenko-ji Temple. As such he is strongly influenced by Muso Soseki, a famous *ishidate-so* (a Zen priest who expressed himself through landscape design)

of the thirteenth century who wrote: 'There is nothing special in water and mountain, there is special only in the mind of people.' For Masuno a garden is a special spiritual place in which the mind dwells and the act of gardening is a personal spiritual training in his quest of a higher understanding of himself. Masuno's design approach

is therefore strongly imbued with the Zen tradition and his gardens embody the essence of this philosophy. Yet in its form and structure this garden also exhibits a very contemporary approach, one that creates thoughtful and contemplative space in the centre of the crematorium.

Hofu City Crematorium, Hofu City, Yamaguchi, Japan, 2003. **Shunmyo Masuno**. b Tsurumi-ku, Yokohama City, Kanagawa, Japan, 1953.

Diana, Princess of Wales Memorial Fountain Gustafson Porter

Kathryn Gustafson and Neil Porter established Gustafson Porter in 1997 and began work on the design of the Diana, Princess of Wales Memorial Fountain in 2003. The tenet of the design is 'Reaching Out–Letting In': the fountain is a focal point within the open landscape of Hyde Park, which simultaneously reaches out and draws people towards it. It is an analogy of two of the Princess's much loved qualities — accessibility and inclusiveness. Oval in shape, the fountain uses existing contours to divert two flows of water downhill in different directions. Central to the impact of the memorial is the range of different types of water movements and the devices that generate these effects. These include jets, bubblers and a fountain, and water cascading over variously textured surfaces and steps all of which create different liquid effects and sounds, and contrast with the placid calm of the reflecting pool at the end of the water's journey.

Diana, Princess of Wales Memorial Fountain, Hyde Park, London, UK, 2004. **Gustafson Porter**. **Kathryn Gustafson**. **b** Yakima, WA, USA, 1951. **Neil Porter**. **b** Epsom, Surrey, UK, 1958. **Mary Bowman**. **b** CA, USA, 1958.

Blue Stick Garden Claude Cormier

A farmer's son from rural Quebec, Claude Cormier studied agronomy, landscape architecture, history and theory of design before founding his own landscape design office in 1995. Cormier's works celebrate man-made nature inasmuch as gardens are manufactured and therefore not natural but artificial. However, his designs begin with the

genius loci — the complex interactions of natural conditions, current and historic socio-political and cultural identity — and result in creations that connect with the human psyche 'physically, sensually, and playfully'. Blue Stick Garden was originally an installation for the inaugural Métis International Garden Festival in 2000, held in the

garden designed by Elsie Reford. In 2004 it travelled to Hestercombe as part of the centenary celebrations of the Arts and Crafts garden designed by Gertrude Jekyll and Sir Edwin Lutyens. Just as Cormier's installation had been inspired by the Himalayan blue poppy which thrives at Métis, so Reford had been inspired by Jekyll.

Blue Stick Garden, Hestercombe Gardens, Taunton, Somerset, UK, 2004. **Claude Cormier. b** Plessisville, QC, Canada, 1960.

Small Tribute to Immigrant Workers Mario Schjetnan

Mario Schjetnan is a Mexican designer and landscape architect who trained in both Mexico and the United States, and was influenced by designers including Barragán, Burle Marx and Halprin. Created as one of the fifteen gardens at the Cornerstone Festival of Gardens in California, Schjetnan's installation has a profound,

moving and hard-hitting message. It is a tribute to those Mexican, often illegal, immigrants without whose hard toil the Californian horticultural industry would not exist. The labyrinth-like entrance creates a sense of the unknown, an emotion keenly felt by those setting off from Mexico for a better life. The flooring of broken crocks symbolizes the

perilous journey to the United States. Inside, visitors can tend the garden of edible crops such as those tended by immigrant workers. While the gabion of caged rocks running along the rear of the installation decorated with photographs of those immigrants who built this garden, represents their strength and that of all immigrant workers.

Small Tribute to Immigrant Workers, Cornerstone Gardens, Sonoma, CA, USA, 2004. **Mario Schjetnan. b** Mexico City, Mexico, 1945.

Glass Bubble Monika Gora

Trained as a landscape architect, Monika Gora established her own practice in 1989, following an extensive period of working and travelling around the world. Such exposure to differing cultures, histories and traditions of garden design and architecture has had a profound impact on her own style. Given a challenging microclimate of hot summers, cold winters, salt-laden winds and tall, shade-giving apartment buildings, Gora wisely and practically decided to create a more conducive environment for plant growth, with a structure that is an intriguing mix of garden, architecture and sculpture. The Glass Bubble is a sheltered garden haven that can be used year-round, filled with exotic, tropical plants. The attractive curvaceous form, which looks like a breaching whale creates a visually arresting and pleasant juxtaposition with the geometric angularity of the surrounding architecture. During the long Swedish winter nights it acts like a welcoming beacon of light and warmth on the shore of Västra Hamnen.

Glass Bubble, Malmö, Sweden, 2006. **Monika Gora. b** Warsaw, Poland, 1959.

Garden for Australia Taylor Cullity Lethlean with Paul Thompson

The design team which prepared the masterplan for this 25-hectare (62-acre) garden consisted of four designers: Kevin Taylor, Kate Cullity, Perry Lethlean and Paul Thompson. Created as part of the Royal Botanic Gardens in Cranbourne, the Garden for Australia is educational and displays the continent's native plants, which vary in their

habitats from tropical jungles through alpine and temperate zones to the most arid desert. In the words of Taylor Cullity Lethlean, the aim is to 'stimulate visitors, in creative landscape compositions, using the diversity and potential of indigenous flora'. The central feature of the garden, the Red Sand Garden, picks up on the colour of Australia's red

soil and is aligned along a north–south axis. The lower half of the image shows the eastern side of the garden where the Rockpool Waterway and five exhibition gardens can be found. On the western side are the contrasting Arid and Dry River gardens alongside the Eucalyptus Walk, which also leads to five 'fingers' of different types of woodland

Garden for Australia, Royal Botanic Gardens, Cranbourne, VIC, Australia, 2006. **Taylor Cullity Lethlean with Paul Thompson**. **Kevin Taylor**. **b** Adelaide, SA, Australia, 1953.   100
Kate Cullity. **b** Perth, WA, Australia, 1956. **Perry Lethlean**. **b** Melbourne, VIC, Australia, 1962. **Paul Thompson**. **b** Melbourne, VIC, Australia, 1945.

Garden of Cosmic Speculation Charles Jencks

This sinuous 120-m- (400-ft-) long terraced earthwork, twisting away from two crescent ponds, here viewed from the top of a snail mound, is the highlight of Charles Jencks's Garden of Cosmic Speculation, begun in Scotland in 1989. Jencks is a passionate advocate of the latest theories about the universe and its history, and several areas of his garden are designed as visual metaphors for scientific theories. The twisting earthwork, for instance, is the most dramatic expression of a fractal — the irregular curves produced by repeated subdivision in mathematics. Its form (but not its meaning) was inspired by the early experiments of Maggie Keswick, Jencks's late wife, into the feng shui principle of laying bare the 'bones of the earth'. Similar ideas occur in other parts of the garden: Jencks has made an unconventional potager called the Physics Garden, comprising six large metal sculptures that represent the double-helix structure of DNA, surrounded by a 'cell wall' of low box and swirling bands of lettuces.

Garden of Cosmic Speculation, Portrack, Dumfries, UK, 1989–2007. Charles Jencks. b Baltimore, MD, USA, 1939.

'In Line of Fire' Topher Delaney

With an eclectic education embracing cultural anthropology, philosophy and landscape architecture, Topher Delaney is a pioneer of what could be termed postmodern Californian garden design. Her work is as thought-provoking as it is innovative and visually striking. Early in her career she decided that gardens were a sculptural form which enabled her to demonstrate her commitment to the environment, 'the perfect combination of art and civic responsibility'. Delaney also considers her works to be about comfort, healing and faith. The 'In Line of Fire' garden is minimalist: the elements perfectly complement the formal rectangular space, emphasizing both the horizontal and vertical planes.

The rough texture of the foliage climbers on one wall contrasts markedly with the smooth, lit glass wall. The tall specimen *Magnolia grandiflora* acts a a focal point to the composition, while the flames introduce a different source of light as well as movement and another contrast, this time with the manicured expanse of gravel.

'In Line of Fire', Private Garden, San Francisco, CA, USA, 2007. **Topher Delaney. b** New York, NY, USA, 1948.

Malibu Beach House Pamela Burton

Pamela Burton, who established her own practice in 1975, has a deep interest in and knowledge of landscape history and its relationship to art, ornamental horticulture and architectural spaces that have symbolic resonance. She draws on these distinct but interrelated disciplines in her designs, to which she also brings a striking and invigorating sense of modern minimalism. The results are garden designs that push forward the discipline of landscape architecture and thus 'provide meaning to the environment'. The open architecture of this beach house blurs into the garden, which, with its sandy paths and water, melds seamlessly to the natural landscape beyond. The composition is typical of Burton's ethos, which considers the 'landscape and architecture as two modes of the same visual and spatial continuum' where the design 'evolves from its cultural and physical environment and is informed by geography, ecology and history'.

Malibu Beach House, Malibu, CA, USA, 2008. **Pamela Burton**. b Santa Monica, CA, USA, 1948.

Glossary

Allée

Straight walk, path or ride bordered by trees or clipped hedges. A series of straight *allées* will often form an ordered geometric pattern.
See pages 5, 6, 14, 30, 74 and 89

Alpines *see* Winter garden

Annuals

Plants (usually, in a garden context, brightly coloured flowers) that live for a single year. They germinate from seed in the spring, are then planted out to flower in summer, then set seed and die as winter approaches. Annuals are the plants most often used in formal carpet-bedding displays.
See page 38

Arboretum

A **botanic garden** for the display of trees and shrubs — often rare native species in danger of being lost or star exotic introductions.
See page 94

Arts and Crafts

Late nineteenth-century British movement, promoted by William Morris, John Ruskin and others, that extolled a return to the perceived values of medieval craftsmanship as a reaction to increasing industrialization. In a garden context, Arts and Crafts style often refers specifically to the work of Jekyll and Lutyens and their followers working in the first two decades of the twentieth century. The dominant approach in twentieth-century garden design worldwide, challenged only in the final decades of the century as the native-plant movement gained influence in the United States, Australia, South Africa, the Middle East and elsewhere.
See pages 85 and 97

Balinese Balé

The Balinese term for an open-air pavilion or elevated platform, sheltered by a roof and supported by pillars. The Balé Bengong is made of four posts, a platform and hip roof, and used traditionally as a retreat from the heat of the day. The Balé Gede is constructed with up to twelve posts and is used for ceremonies and banquets.
See page 92

Bassin

A formal pool, often stone-edged and/or with a fountain at its centre, and usually part of a formal plan.

Bosco

A grove of trees or a wood, natural or man-made, often incorporated into the design of an Italian Renaissance garden. Wilder in aspect than a ***bosquet*** and frequently sited on a mount.

Bosquet

A small clump of trees, or a decorative glade with statuary, enclosed by a hedge or fence, usually a part of a seventeenth- or eighteenth-century French formal landscape.
See pages 30 and 89

Botanic garden

A representative collection of plants, from a particular geographic location or specific botanical groups (rare and exotic examples such as orchids, ferns, rhododendrons) for which, especially during the eighteenth and nineteenth centuries, plant hunters gathered new and rare species on expeditions abroad. Increasingly, motivated by scientific reasons rather than perpetuating the private collection as a status symbol of the wealthy.
See pages 13, 67 and 100

Carpet bedding

Nineteenth-century practice of planting out young seedlings of **annual** plants *en masse* to create abstract effects based on masses of colours. A technique still used widely in municipal parks worldwide.

Contextual

Designed to relate to or imitate its context or setting.

English landscape style

Garden design style formulated during the first years of the eighteenth century, first as an art form analogous to literature, with complex symbolic and political meanings expressed as buildings and landscape features. Later, it became a purely visual or painterly medium, evocative of a pastoral idyll — as with the work of Capability Brown. A style reproduced throughout Europe in the eighteenth and nineteenth centuries.

Fête champêtre

A large-scale open-air party, often requiring guests to wear fancy dress or masks, and usually in the grounds of a large country house with a variety of diversions for the party-goers. Louis XIV's *fêtes champêtres* at Versailles were probably the most sumptuous events ever seen.
See page 89

Folly

A built structure whose principal purpose is decorative or whimsical rather than practical; occasionally a utility building made to look like a historic, ruined or fantastical structure.
See page 54

Garden cemeteries

Landscape style developed in the nineteenth century, in which cemeteries were designed with as much care as rustic parks. Later, in the United States and elsewhere, the forest cemetery was developed. Examples include the Tulcán Gardens in Ecuador, the Woodland Cemetery in Sweden and the Garden of Rest for the Brion-Vega Tomb in the cemetery of San Vito d'Altivole in Italy.
See pages 21, 22 and 48

Gazon coupé

Grass with shapes cut out of turf and filled with coloured earths or gravels. Used principally in England in the seventeenth century for formal **parterre** designs.

Grotto

A cave-like room usually man-made, decorated with shells, minerals and fossils. Italian Renaissance grottoes were semi-open structures set in the open garden. Later, in eighteenth-century England, grottoes began to be made as discrete buildings — sometimes underground — lined with shells and minerals.
See pages 39 and 51

Heempark, Heemtuin

Dutch park or garden planted with native flora; dates from the 1920s.

Herbaceous border

Areas that consist entirely of **perennial** plants that die back to an underground root every winter, then re-grow in spring. In practice, most 'herbaceous' borders are in fact mixed borders: i.e. they also contain evergreens, bulbs and **annuals**.
See pages 11, 38, 45, 55, 61, 68 and 76

Knot Garden

An enclosed garden, based on Tudor precedents, comprising low evergreen hedges, usually box, yew, or thyme, planted to create an intricate and pleasing symmetrical pattern, sometimes with infills of brightly coloured flowers or gravel.

Landscape style *see* English landscape style

Latin plant names

The two-word plant-naming system was devised by Swedish botanist Linnaeus (hence the Linnean system) in the eighteenth century. The first word is the genus; the second is the species. The system is useful as it is precise, accurate and international. However, it means that plant names can be hard to pronounce and difficult to remember.

Modernism

Style formulated in the 1920s, characterized by architecture that could be mass-produced and the use of modern materials such as concrete. The 'white-cube' building is an archetypal Modernist style. A variety of garden styles have been used in an attempt to complement the building style.
See pages 5, 6, 7, 9, 12, 15, 20, 30, 32, 34, 37, 38, 41, 58, 60, 68, 70, 83, 84, 85, 88 and 93

Native plants

Plants that naturally occur in the wild in a given area. In nineteenth-century horticulture the emphasis was on recently introduced exotic plants, but from the late twentieth century there has been increasing interest in native flora and this has impacted on design.
See pages 4, 35, 46, 51, 61, 88, 91 and 100

New Perennial movement/style

A naturalistic planting style composed of big and bold drifts of hardy **perennials** and ornamental grasses. Most effective on a large scale, it is a concept that has the benefit of being low maintenance.
See pages 55 and 88

Objet trouvé

From the French for 'found object'. The integration into the garden's design of objects of daily use such as mirrors or crockery and natural shells or stones goes back to the Renaissance and flourished in Baroque and Rococo gardens. In more recent times, however, it became the hallmark of the fantastic environments created by self-taught eccentrics or 'outsider' artists. Elements can be seen in Derek Jarman's Prospect Cottage.
See page 59

Pallissade

A clipped hedge, often hornbeam, constituting a green wall to line an **allée**.
See page 45

Parterre

Formal terrace decorated in one of a variety of styles, from simple patterns of cut turf and gravel (**gazon coupé**) to intricate designs made of hedges, grass, gravel, turf and flowers (*parterre de broderie*).
See pages 4, 6, 39 and 74

Patio

Traditionally, a small, paved Spanish courtyard surrounded by an arcade, often filled with potted plants.
See pages 34, 42, 49 and 65

Perennials *see* Herbaceous border

Pergola

Wooden and/or stone structure that forms a covered walkway, often planted with climbers such as roses, vines or wisteria.
See page 63

Picturesque

Late eighteenth-century landscape style (almost exclusively English) that celebrates the power of untamed nature, frequently in a setting of extreme terrain. Loosely used to describe the **English landscape style** in Europe. The term comes from the idea of making landscapes in the manner of pictures.

Plantsman, -woman

An expert in garden plants and gardening, or a particular style of garden where planting and the use of plants is a defining feature or an intrinsic part of its design.
See pages 53 and 66

Rill

With their origins in early Persian gardens, a rill is a narrow, shallow man-made stream or rivulet, usually lined with stone, and used on a gentle gradient to convey water from one area of the garden to another. Rills can be serpentine like Ron Lutsko's Sustainability Gardens at Turtle Bay, or linear as used by Sir Edwin Lutyens and Gertrude Jekyll in their **Arts and Crafts** gardens.
See page 93

Serpentine paths

Curving or twisting paths running through areas of shrub and tree planting. Serpentine paths frequently lend a note of informality to otherwise symmetrical schemes. Examples include Ron Lutsko's Sustainability Gardens at Turtle Bay and Andy Goldsworthy's 'Taking a Wall for a Walk'.
See pages 64 and 93

Shakkei/Chie ching

In both Japanese (*shakkei*) and Chinese garden (*chie ching*) design traditions, a technique which consists of 'borrowing' a particular landscape or part of a landscape into the garden composition. An application of scroll-painting techniques, the 'borrowing' is achieved by playing on the various parts or 'layers' of a view (foreground, middle ground and background). It is different from the Western use of vistas or surrounding landscape in the same way as a landscape painting is unlike a Japanese or Chinese landscape scroll.

Stroll garden

A Japanese style of garden, popular from the thirteenth century, which is designed to be viewed while walking following a particular path. The garden is then revealed gradually in a sequence of views, ambience and perspectives. It is reminiscent of the act of looking at a long Oriental scroll landscape painting. It usually involves a circuit around a lake with various tea arbours, bridges and islands.
See page 79

Tapis vert

Literally, a green carpet: a close cropped expanse of grass — usually part of a formal scheme.
See page 30

Topiary

The art of clipping evergreen plants, such as box and yew, into abstract or figurative shapes.
See pages 11 and 21

Trompe-l'oeil

From the French 'deceive the eye'. An effect designed to alter normal perception. Often used in gardens to increase distances and change perspectives. It can take the form of out-of-scale plantings, trellises, mirrors or even painted surfaces.
See page 73

Wilderness

Enclosed, informal areas in a landscape garden, planted with trees and shrubs and featuring **serpentine** walks.
See page 93

Winter garden

Alpine or rock garden, or an indoor heated conservatory for the display of exotic plants.
See pages 38, 67 and 100

Directory

Garden opening times vary throughout the year and access may be limited during restoration work. It is advisable to check the dates and times of opening prior to visiting or making travel arrangements. Private gardens are not listed unless they are open to the public.

Australia

Garden for Australia 2006
Royal Botanic Gardens,
Cranbourne, VIC
Open daily except Christmas Day,
9am to 5pm
Guided tours available
www.rbg.vic.gov.au/australian_garden

Czech Republic

University Botanic Garden and Arboretum 1990s
Mendel University of Agriculture & Forestry, Brno
Open Mon to Fri, 7am to 3pm
wwwold.mendelu.cz/arboretum

Denmark

University of Aarhus 1953
Aarhus
Grounds open to the public
www.au.dk

Ecuador

Tulcán Gardens 1940s
Tulcán
Open to the public

Finland

Villa Mairea 1939
Noormarkku
Open only by appointment
www.villamairea.fi

France

Château de Chaumont-sur-Loire
Ferme du château, Chaumont-sur-Loire
Annual festival open daily, 30 Apr to 19 Oct, 9.30am to dusk
www.chaumont-jardins.com

The Labyrinth 1968
Fondation Maeght, Saint-Paul
Open daily, Oct to June, 10am to 6pm; Jul to Sept, 10am to 7pm
www.fondation-maeght.com

Parc André Citroën 1992
Quai André Citroën, Paris
Open to the public

Parc de la Villette 1982
Avenue Jean Jaurès, Paris
Open daily, 9.30am to 6.30pm
www.villette.com

UNESCO Foundation Sculpture Garden 1958
Place de Fontenoy, Paris
Open Mon to Fri, 9.30am to 12.30pm & 2.30pm to 6pm
Closed public holidays
www.unesco.org

Villa Noailles 1926
Montée de Noailles, Hyères
Open daily July to Sept (except Tues), 10am to 12pm & 4pm to 7.30pm; Jan to June & Oct to Dec (except Mon & Tues), 10am to 12.30pm & 2pm to 5.30pm
www.villanoailles-hyeres.com

Villa Savoye 1931
Chemin de Villiers, Poissy
Open daily except Mon, Mar to Apr & Sept to Oct, 10am to 5pm; May to Aug, 10am to 6pm; Nov to Feb, 10am to 1pm & 2pm to 5pm
Closed on 1 Jan, 1 May, 1 & 11 Nov & 25 Dec
villa-savoye.monuments-nationaux.fr

India

Rock Garden 1950s
Chandigarh
Open daily, Apr to Sept, 9am to 7pm; Oct to Mar, 9am to 6pm
www.nekchand.com

Italy

Garden of Rest, Brion-Vega Tomb 1978
Cemetery of San Vito d'Altivole, Treviso
Open to the public

The Tarot Garden 1998
Pescia Fiorentina, Capalbio, Grosseto
Open daily, 1 Apr to 15 Oct, 2.30pm to 7.30pm
www.nikidesaintphalle.com

Villa il Roseto 1965
The Michelucci Foundation, Fiesole, Florence
Open weekdays, 9am to 1pm
www.michelucci.it

Japan

Garden of Fine Arts 1994
Kyoto National Museum
Open daily except Mon, 9am to 4.30pm
www.kyohaku.go.jp

Site of Reversible Destiny 1995
Yoro Park, Kyoto
Open daily except Mon, 9am to 5pm
Closed 29 Dec to 3 Jan
www.yoro-park.com

Tofuku-ji 1939
Kyoto
Open daily, Dec to Oct, 9am to 4pm; Nov, 8.30am to 4.30pm
www.tofukuji.jp

Netherlands

Kröller-Müller Sculpture Park 1961
Houtkampweg, Otterlo
Open daily except Mon, 10am to 4.30pm; closed 1 Jan
www.kmm.nl

Kwekerij Oudolf 1982
Hummelo, Arnhem
Open Tues to Sat, Apr to June & Aug to Oct, first weekend in Sept & Oct, 10am to 4pm
Check website for special open days
www.oudolf.com

Mien Ruys Tuinen 1990
Dedemsvaart
Open daily except Mon, Apr to Oct, 10am to 5pm; Sun, 12pm to 5pm
www.mienruys.nl/

Romania

Târgu Jiu Sculpture Park 1938
Open to the public
www.targujiu.ro

Spain

German Pavilion (Barcelona Pavilion) 1929
Montjuïc, Barcelona
Open daily, 10am to 8pm
Guided tours, Wed & Fri, 5pm to 7pm
www.miesbcn.com

Sweden

Woodland Cemetery 1940
Enskede, Stockholm
Open to the public
www.skogskyrkogarden.se

Switzerland

Uetliberg Garden c1980
Zürich
Open to the public

UK

Barbara Hepworth Museum & Sculpture Garden 1975
Barnoon Hill, St Ives, Cornwall
Open daily, Mar to Oct, 10am to 5.20pm; open Nov to Feb, Tues to Sun, 10am to 4.20pm (or dusk)
www.tate.org.uk/stives

Chelsea Flower Show
Royal Hospital, Chelsea
Annual event, see website for details
www.rhs.org.uk/chelsea

Dartington Hall 1945
Totnes, Devon
Gardens open daily, dawn to dusk
Tours by appointment, see website for further details
www.dartingtonhall.com

Denmans 1980
Fontwell, West Sussex
Open daily, 9am to 5pm (or dusk)
www.denmans-garden.co.uk

Diana, Princess of Wales Memorial Fountain 2004
Hyde Park, London
Open daily, Apr to Aug, 10am to 8pm; Sept, 10am to 7pm; Mar and Oct, 10am to 6pm; Nov to Feb, 10am to 4pm
www.royalparks.org.uk/parks/hyde_park/diana_memorial.cfm

Eden Project 2001
Bodelva, St Austell, Cornwall
Open daily, summer, 10am to 6pm; winter, 10am to 4.30pm
Closed Christmas Eve & Christmas Day
www.edenproject.com

Garden of Cosmic Speculation 2007
Portrack, Dumfries
Open occasionally through Scotland's Gardens Scheme
www.gardensofscotland.org

The Gibberd Garden 1956
Harlow, Essex
Open Apr to Sep, Wed, Sat, Sun & Bank Holidays, 2pm to 6pm
www.thegibberdgarden.co.uk

Little Sparta 1966
Dunsyre, Lanarkshire
Open 15 June to 28 Sept, Wed, Fri & Sun, 2.30 to 5pm
www.littlesparta.co.uk

Perry Green 1940
The Henry Moore Foundation, Much Hadham, Hertfordshire
Open only by appointment
Closed Mon & Bank Holidays
www.henry-moore-fdn.co.uk

Sutton Place 1986
Sutton Park, Sutton Green, Guildford, Surrey
Open only by appointment for pre-booked parties

'Taking a Wall for a Walk' 1990
Grizedale Forest Park, Hawkshead, Ambleside, Cumbria
Visitor centre open daily, 14 July to 7 Sept, 10am to 5.30pm; 8 Sept to 2 Nov, 10am to 5.00pm; 3 Nov to 30 Nov, 10am to 4.30pm, 1 Dec to 23 Dec, 10am to 4pm
www.forestry.gov.uk/forestry/infd-5k2b6b

Turn End 1964
Townside, Haddenham, Aylesbury, Buckinghamshire
Open occasionally through the National Gardens Scheme
www.ngs.org.uk

USA

MoMA Courtyard Sculpture Gaden (The Abby Aldrich Rockefeller Sculpture Garden) 1953
New York, NY
Open Wed to Mon, 10.30am to 5.30pm; Fri, 10.30am to 8pm
www.moma.org

Cornerstone Gardens
Sonoma, CA
Open daily, 10am to 4pm
www.cornerstonegardens.com

Fallingwater 1939
Bear Run, PA
Open daily except Wed, Mar to Thanksgiving weekend, Dec weekends, Christmas week and the first two weekends in Mar, 10am to 4pm; Easter Sunday, Memorial Day, 4 July, Labor Day, Columbus Day, Thanksgiving Friday, 1pm to 4pm; Closed Jan & Feb
Guided tours available
www.fallingwater.org

The James Rose Center 1954
East Ridgewood Avenue,
Ridgewood, NJ
Open daily, 15 May to 1 Sept
Self-guided tours available,
Mon to Fri, 10am to 4pm
www.jamesrosecenter.org

Lincoln Memorial Garden 1949
East Lake Drive, Springfield, IL
Open daily (closed public holidays),
sunrise to sunset
www.lmgnc.org

LongHouse Reserve 1986
East Hampton, NY
Open end Apr to Sept, Wed & Sat,
2pm to 5pm
www.longhouse.org

Naumkeag 1925
Prospect Hill, Stockbridge, MA
Open Memorial Day to Columbus Day,
10am to 5pm
Guided tours available
www.thetrustees.org/pages/
335_naumkeag.cfm

**Sustainability Gardens at
Turtle Bay** 2003
Redding, CA
Open daily, Mar to Oct, 9am to 5pm;
Nov to Feb, 9am to 5pm
Closed Tues, Thanksgiving day,
Christmas day and New Year's day
www.turtlebay.org

Index

The entries in **bold** are the garden-makers and gardens featured in this book.

Acknowledgements

Texts written by Barbara Abbs, Patrick Bowe, Kathryn Bradley-Hole, Anne de Charmant, Aulani Mulford, Toby Musgrave, Jennifer Potter and Tim Richardson.

Photographic Credits

AKG, London/Erich Lessing: 10; © Mark Bolton Photography/Alamy: 97; The Art Archive: 14; Richard Barnes: 98; Bastin & Evrard: 71; Bibliothèque nationale de France, Paris: 5, 6; Helene Binet: 96; Luc Boegly/Archipress: 32; © Bruce Botnick 2007: 103; Nicola Browne: 55, 56; Nicola Browne/New Eden/IPC Syndication: 68; Karl-Dietrich Buhler/www.elizabethwhiting.com: 39; A E Bye: 46; Dean Cardasis: 81; Dixi Carillo: 74; © Fernando Caruncho: 69; Frederick Charles: 29; Martin Charles: 20; Jean Loup Charmet: 4, 7; Charles Chesshire: 79; Child Associates: 80; © Peter Cook: 16; Country Life Picture Library: 11, 15; Country Life Picture Library/Clive Boursnell: 22, 40, 45, 60; Country Life Picture Library/John Frost: 12; Country Life Picture Library/Alex Ramsey: 78; Country Life Picture Library/Vivian Russell: 9; Jerôme Darblay: 41; Ken Druse: 57; Garrett

Eckbo Collection (1990–1) Environmental Design Archives, University of California, Berkley: 33; Richard Felber: 66; © Lucas Fladzinski: 102; Courtesy of Fondation Maeght, Photo: Claude Germain: 43; Garden Matters: 8, 23; John Glover: 85; Mick Hales: 24; Lars Hallén/Design Press: 18; Harpur Garden Library/Jerry Harpur: 35, 49, 58, 61, 87; Harpur Garden Library/Marcus Harpur: 31; Reproduced by permission of the Henry Moore Foundation, Photograph Michael Furze: 19; Marijke Heuff: 63; Juergen Holzenleuchter. 50; © 2008 Digital Image, Timothy Hursley/The Museum of Modern Art, New York/Scala, Firenze: 28; Peter Hyatt:100; Imagination Limited: 91; Interior Archive/Jacques Dirand/Inside: 89; Interior Archive/Helen Fickling: 51; Interior Archive/Celia Innes: 65; Donald Jensen/Saritaksu: 92; Stephen Jerrom: 90; Photograph Nitin Kevalkar/Images of India/Dinodia Picture Agency: 25; Balthazar Korab: 30; Courtesy of the Kröller-Müller Museum: 36; Michele Lamontagne: 17; The Landscape Institute/BCA: 44; Courtesy of Bernard Lassus: 73; Andrew Lawson: 38, 64, 70, 83, 94; Jannes Linders: 77;

Åke E:son Lindman: 99; Marianne Majerus: 72, 101; Mayer/Lescanff: 54; Tabata Minao: 95; Tony Morrison/South American Pictures: 21; The National Archives, UK, [work 25/211]: 26; Clive Nichols: 88; Ivar Otruba: 67; Photolibrary/Garden Picture Library/Nigel Francis: 13; Photolibrary/Garden Picture Library/Michel Viard: 53; RIBA Library Photographs Collection: 37; Courtesy of The Royal Danish Academy of Fine Arts, School of Architecture: 27; Deidi von Schaewen: 86; Mark Schwartz: 84; Everett H Scott: 18; William Shaw/New Eden: 76; Shinkenchiku-sha: 75; Ezra Stoller © Esto: 34; Tim Street-Porter: 42, 62; Shodo Suzuki: 52; Curtice Taylor/Conran Octopus: 59; Patrick Taylor: 47; Photo: Heidrun Weiler: 82; © 2008 Steve Whittaker: 93

Jacket: photo by Mark Schwartz

All reasonable efforts have been made to trace the copyright holders of the photographs used in this book. We apologize to anyone that we have been unable to reach.

Phaidon Press Limited
Regent's Wharf
All Saints Street
London N1 9PA

Phaidon Press Inc.
180 Varick Street
New York, NY 10014

www.phaidon.com

First published as *The Garden
Book* 2000
This edition abridged, revised and
updated 2009
© 2000, 2009 Phaidon Press Limited

ISBN 978 0 7148 4958 4

A CIP catalogue record for this book
is available from the British Library.

Designed by Susanne Olsson
Printed in China